Hodder Comprehension

an integrated, skills-based approach

BOOK SIX

Janice Cunningham, Sharon Hayles,
Gladys Morgan, Karen Morrison and Daphne Paizee

HODDER
EDUCATION
AN HACHETTE UK COMPANY

The Publishers would like to thank the following for permission to reproduce copyright material:
Photo credits
page 10: Bigstock (left); Alamy/Afripics.com (right)
page 13: Topfoto/INPRA
page 23: The Bigger Picture/Reuters
page 25: The Bigger Picture/Reuters
page 27: The Bigger Picture/Reuters
page 35: The Bigger Picture/Reuters
page 36: Reuters/Kai Pfaffenbach
page 50: Mike van der Wolk (mike@springhigh.co.za)
page 55: Mike van der Wolk (mike@springhigh.co.za)
page 64: Alamy/Afripics.com (left); Bigstock (right)
page 65: Greatstock/Corbis (left); The Bigger Picture/Reuters (right)
page 92: Greatstock/Corbis (top); Topfoto/INPRA (bottom)
page 93: Greatstock/Corbis
page 104: The Bigger Picture/Reuters
Acknowledgements
page 2: "The mouse" © Karen Morrison.
page 2: "Mice" by Rose Fyleman, with permissions from The Society of Authors, on behalf of the Estate of Rose Fyleman.
page 11: "Willow and Ginkgo" by Eve Merriam, from *A sky full of poems* by Eve Merriam. Full name of the poem: "Simile: Willow and Ginkgo". Copyright © 1964, 1970, 1973, 1986 Eve Merriam. Used by permission of Marian Reiner.
page 13: Edward Lear
page 14: Edward Lear
page 15: Edward Lear
page 26: 1GOAL is a campaign of the Global Campaign for Education (GCE), a civil society network of campaigning organisations, teachers' unions and NGOs operational in over 100 countries. GCE campaigns to ensure that governments act now to deliver the right of everyone to a free quality public education. 1GOAL information reproduced courtesy of the Global Campaign for Education.
page 53: Cover from *The Great Kapok Tree: A Tale of the Amazon Rain Forest* by Lynne Cherry, copyright © 1990 by Lynne Cherry. Reprinted by permission of Houghton Mifflin Harcourt Publishing Company. All rights reserved.
page 91: "My car is constructed of pickles" by Kenn Nesbitt, © Sourcebooks Jabberwocky 2009: *My hippo has the hiccups: and other poems I totally made up* by Kenn Nesbitt.
page 103: Taken from Evalyn Parry's song *Instructions for learning to ride a bicycle, by Miss Frances Willard, 1895*, © Evalyn Parry (SOCAN), lyrics adapted from text by Frances Willard's "A Wheel within A Wheel".
pages 3, 17, 19, 20 and 21: All poems on these pages © Karen Morrison.

Orders: please contact Bookpoint Ltd, 130 Milton Park, Abingdon, Oxon OX14 4SB. Telephone: (44) 01235 827720. Fax: (44) 01235 400454. Lines are open 9.00–5.00, Monday to Saturday, with a 24-hour message answering service. Visit our website at www.hoddereducation.com.

First published in 2012 by
Hodder Education, an Hachette UK Company,
338 Euston Road
London NW1 3BH

Impression number 5 4 3 2
Year 2016 2015 2014 2013

Teacher's notes: Jan Gallow
Project management: Sally Howes
Editing: Ilse Badenhorst
Illustrations: Tinny Rosser, Vian Oelofsen and Johann Strauss
Cover illustration: Alzette Prins
Typeset in RuimStoneSans 13 pt by Baseline Publishing Services, Cape Town
Printed in Dubai

A catalogue record for this title is available from the British Library

ISBN 978 1444 15033 9

Contents

We are here to help you through this book. Look out for us!

Rachel Benita Petula Xavier Shawn Ricardo

1 Animal poetry

Before you begin

- Think about a poem you have read or heard and enjoyed. Answer these questions about the poem.
  - What was the poem about?
  - Who wrote the poem?
  - What made you like it?
  - How did the poem make you feel?
  - What is your favourite line from the poem?
- Work with a partner and tell each other about your favourite poems.

1. Here are three poems about mice. Read the poems with a partner and then answer the questions.

The mouse

All dressed in grey,
A little mouse
Has made his home
Within my house.
And every night,
And every morn
I say, "I wish
That mouse were gone."
But why?
A quiet soul is he
As anyone might wish to see.
My house is large,
My hearth is wide,
There's room for him
And me beside.

Mice
by Rose Fyleman

I think mice
are rather nice.
Their tails are long,
Their faces small,
They haven't any
Chins at all.

Their ears are pink,
Their teeth are white.
They run around
The house at night.

They nibble things
They shouldn't touch
And no one seems
To like them much.

But I think mice
are nice.

 SKILLS: Discuss a familiar poem. Read poems.

A mouse in my house

Help! There's a mouse.
Get it out of my house.

They're disgusting
They're dirty,
Their fur's full of fleas
And I am quite sure
That they might spread disease.

Stamp your feet
Make a noise
Go fetch a broom
But whatever you do
Get it out of my room!

a. Which poem do you like best? Why?

b. Each poem has a different way of rhyming. Underline the rhyming words in each poem.

c. Describe the rhyming pattern in each poem.
The mouse:
Mice:
A mouse in my house:

2. Read this poem silently on your own. Then answer the questions on page 5.

The donkey

I saw a donkey,
One day old,
His head was too big
For his neck to hold;
His legs were shaky
And long and loose.
They rocked and staggered
And weren't much use.

He tried to gambol
And frisk a bit,
But he wasn't quite sure
Of the trick of it.
His queer little coat
Was soft and grey,
And it curled at his neck
In a lovely way.

He looked so little
And weak and slim,
I prayed the world
Might be good to him.

a. Was the poem easy to read and understand? Give a reason for your answer.

b. Is this poem suitable for your age group or is it too simple? Give a reason for your answer.

c. What do these words from the poem mean?
  - rocked:
  - staggered:
  - gambol:
  - frisk:

d. Write down one word that describes the feeling of this poem.

e. What did you like best about this poem?

f. What did you not like about it?

g. No one knows who wrote this poem. But if you could meet the person who wrote it, what would you ask him or her about the poem? Think of at least three questions.

3. The poem "The donkey" describes a new-born donkey. A baby donkey is called a foal. What do you call the following animal babies?
   a. A baby cat is a
   b. A baby dog is a
   c. A baby bear is a
   d. A baby cow is a
   e. A baby sheep is a
   f. A baby bird is a
   g. A baby lion is a
   h. A baby whale is a

SKILLS: Answer questions. Justify opinions. Define words. Write questions. Identify young animals.

4. a. Work with a partner. Read through these instructions for learning and performing a poem.

How to perform a poem

1. Try to learn the poem off by heart. The better you know it, the better your performance will be.
2. If you have to read the poem, read slowly and clearly, looking up at your audience as often as you can. Use your hands if possible and change the expression on your face.
3. If the poem has a special rhythm, practise reading it and saying it until you get it right. Think about clicking your fingers, beating the rhythm on a table or using an instrument to match the rhythm of the poem.
4. Think about the message of the poem and match the tone of the poem with your voice and expressions. Do not smile and use a happy tone if the poem is sad.
5. Practise your performance until you are happy with it. Ask a partner to listen to your performance and to give you feedback before you perform it for the whole class (or school).

b. How would you add to or adapt these instructions if the poem were going to be performed by a small group instead of one person? Write your ideas here.

5. Read this poem quietly on your own and then answer the questions.

A cat and a mouse and a bumblebee

A cat and a mouse and a bumblebee
Started a-dancing, one, two, three.
They danced in the daytime,
They danced in the night,
They cared not whether it was dark or light.

What did they dance to? Don't ask me!
They danced to the hum of the bumblebee.
They danced to the purr of the big tom-cat,
They danced to the mouse-squeaks high as a bat.

Where did they go to? I don't know!
Nobody ever saw them go.
But if you ask me,
I'm willing to bet
That if they're alive they are dancing yet.

a. Do you think the poet is describing a real experience? Give reasons for your answers.

b. How would you recite this poem? Would you speak softly or loudly, quickly or slowly? Why?

c. What was the poet feeling when the poem was written?

6. Prepare to perform this poem. Your teacher will choose some pupils to perform it for the class.

2 Figures of speech

Before you begin

- Work in small groups. Try to say these tongue twisters five times in a row as fast as you can. Try not to stumble or hesitate.

- Why is it difficult to say these phrases over and over?
- Do you know any other tongue twisters? Share them with your group.

Alliteration

Alliteration is the use of two or more words in a row which start with the same sound. All of the tongue twisters above use alliteration. Poets use alliteration for effect, for example, the clouds drifted dreamily downwards or her shrill shrieks tore the silence to shreds.

1. Underline the alliteration in these lines of poetry. Then say each line out loud.
   a. Flickering flames fanned by the wild, whooshing wind.
   b. Dolphins dancing from dawn to dusk.
   c. Dewdrops dancing on daisies.
   d. Careless cars cutting corners, creating chaos.
   e. William's wise words echoed, teasing Tessa's brain.
   f. Rudolph the red-nosed reindeer.

2. Compose a sentence about each of these topics. Your sentences should all have some alliteration in them.
   a. alligators: ______
   b. babies: ______
   c. loud music: ______
   d. spiders: ______
   e. rain: ______
   f. swimming: ______
   g. the wind: ______
   h. a dentist: ______

 SKILLS: Say, identify, interpret and write examples of alliteration.

3. Companies often use alliteration in their advertisements to catch your attention and make it easier for you to remember their brands. For example: Billy's bed, bath and beyond or Betty's best buys. Write down one example of alliteration associated with the following products.
   a. doughnuts: ______
   b. patties: ______
   c. cola: ______
   d. books: ______
   e. cheese: ______
   f. airlines: ______

4. Singers, actors and even cartoon characters often have names that have alliteration. The alliteration makes the name stand out and makes it easier for you to remember. Think about Donald Duck, Mickey Mouse and SpongeBob SquarePants. Now make up a stage name with alliteration in it for the following first names.
   a. Peter: ______
   b. Marilyn: ______
   c. Jack: ______
   d. Angie: ______
   e. Wendell: ______
   f. Salma: ______

5. Many sayings and idioms also use alliteration. Underline the sayings and then write down what each one means.
   a. He is a real busy bee. ______
   b. Benita had the last laugh. ______
   c. Mr Jones has retired well and he is living life to the fullest. ______
   d. Mary is a real moaning Minnie. ______
   e. I feel right as rain this morning. ______
   f. He looks smart, but fine feathers do not make fine birds. ______
   g. My granny always says speech is silver, silence is golden. ______

SKILLS: Say, identify, interpret and write examples of alliteration.

Similes

A simile is a direct comparison between two things. In a simile, the comparison is always introduced using the words like or as. For example:

- The shadows were striped like tigers.
- The girls sneaked into the room as silently as the night.

Poets use similes for effect and to help us paint mental pictures of things.

6. Use your own ideas to complete these similes.
   a. He wandered as lonely as a ________________
   b. She ran as fast as ________________
   c. The moon looked like a ________________
   d. The boy's face was as pale as ________________
   e. Her hair looked like a ________________
   f. He screamed like a ________________

7. Look at the photographs below of two different types of trees.
   a. How are the trees similar?

   ____

   ____

   b. How are the trees different?

   ____

   ____

This is a willow tree. These trees are also known as weeping willows.

This is a ginkgo tree. These trees are also known as maidenhair trees.

 SKILLS: Read and write similes. Analyse and compare photographs.

8. Read this poem called "Willow and Ginkgo". Pay attention to the comparisons that the poet makes and then answer the questions.

Willow and Ginkgo
by Eve Merriam

The willow is like an etching,
Fine-lined against the sky.
The ginkgo is like a crude sketch,
Hardly worthy to be signed.
The willow's music is like a soprano,
Delicate and thin.
The ginkgo's tune is like a chorus
With everyone joining in.

The willow is sleek as a velvet-nosed calf;
The ginkgo is leathery as an old bull.
The willow's branches are like silken thread;
The ginkgo's like stubby rough wool.

The willow is like a nymph with streaming hair;
Wherever it grows, there is green and gold and fair.
The willow dips to the water,
Protected and precious, like the king's favourite daughter.

The ginkgo forces its way through grey concrete;
Like a city child, it grows up in the street.
Thrust against the metal sky,
Somehow it survives and even thrives.
My eyes feast upon the willow,
But my heart goes to the ginkgo.

a. Use red to underline all the similes that compare the willow to something else.
b. Use blue to underline all the similes that compare the ginkgo to something else.
c. Which simile in the poem do you like best? Write it here.

____

d. Why does this comparison appeal to you?

____

____

Metaphors

A metaphor is an indirect comparison. The comparison is suggested rather than stated, so it does not have the comparison words like or as.
For example:

- Life is a rollercoaster.
- My grandpa is a bear of a man.
- The sea is a large green snake against the sand.

9. Underline the metaphors in the following sentences. Below each one say which things are being compared.
   a. My sister is a slug. She hates getting out of bed.

   ____

   b. The storm has made the sea a hungry brown bear.

   ____

   c. The class were an obedient flock of sheep, following their teacher to the park.

   ____

   d. Her eyes were emeralds and her lips were rubies.

   ____

10. Say whether each of these sentences is an example of a simile or a metaphor.
   a. The moon is a ghostly galleon. _______________
   b. I wandered lonely as a cloud. _______________
   c. Like the park birds he came early. _______________
   d. A whole trainful of coal, like a soul burnt black in a hole. _______________
   e. Like a bundle of old rope and iron. _______________
   f. His hair is an exclamation mark. _______________
   g. Ears like bombs and teeth like splinters. _______________
   h. I rolled away safe as Elijah. _______________
   i. As cool as the pale wet leaves. _______________
   j. She is my sky, my air, my breath. _______________

3 A story poem

Before you begin

- Learn this verse and say it aloud as a class.

The Jumblies
by Edward Lear

Far and few, far and few
Are the lands where the Jumblies live;
Their heads are green and their hands are blue
And they went to sea in a sieve.

> **The Jumblies**
> "The Jumblies" is a nonsense poem written by a poet called Edward Lear. He is famous for his light-hearted and humorous poetry. In this section you are going to learn about the poet and then study one of his best-known poems in detail.

- Draw a few Jumblies based on the image you have from the poem.

1. Skim read this biographical information about Edward Lear.

Edward Lear

Edward Lear was a British poet and painter who became known for his funny and witty poems. Born in 1812, he was the youngest of 21 children. Edward was educated at home by his older sister Anne. She was 21 years older than he was.

His father, Jeremiah, was a stockbroker who became bankrupt when Edward was only 13. His father was sent to debtors' prison and Edward was forced to work to earn a living and help the family.

Edward was a talented artist and he got a job at the London Zoological Society, where he made beautiful coloured drawings of parrots. He quickly became well known for his work and he was invited by Lord Stanley, the Earl of Denby, to live on his estate and draw the birds in his collection. Lear lived there for about six years, and in that time, he composed his first book of poems. The collection, called *A Book of Nonsense* (1846), was written for Lord Stanley's grandchildren.

When he left the Denby estate, Lear travelled all over Europe and Asia, where he concentrated on painting. He also wrote several travel journals, which he illustrated. These were published in England.

Although he was a great artist, Lear is best know for his poems. He is also credited with being the creator of the limerick. He died in 1888 at the age of 76.

2. Answer these questions about Edward Lear's life.
   a. When and where was Edward Lear born?
   b. How old was he when he began to work for a living?
   c. What was his first job?
   d. What was the title of his first book of poetry?
   e. Did Lear publish other books?
   f. Which type of short poem did Lear invent?
   g. When did Edward Lear die?

3. Read this limerick by Edward Lear.

The lady of Firle
by Edward Lear

There was a young lady of Firle
Whose hair was addicted to curl;
It curled up a tree
And all over the sea
That expansive young lady of Firle.

   a. Discuss the structure of a limerick with your partner.
      - How many lines does it have?
      - Which lines rhyme?
      - What is the rhythm of a limerick?
   b. Draw a fun picture to illustrate the limerick above.
   c. Complete this limerick.

There was a young boy from Peru
Who really liked to eat stew;
He ______________________
So ______________________
And ended up eating his shoe.

 SKILLS: Answer questions. Read and discuss a limerick. Draw a picture. Complete a limerick.

4. "The Owl and the Pussycat" is one of Edward Lear's best-known lyrical story poems. Read it through twice on your own.

The owl and the pussycat
by Edward Lear

The Owl and the Pussycat went to sea
In a beautiful pea-green boat,
They took some honey, and plenty of money,
Wrapped up in a five pound note.
The Owl looked up to the stars above,
And sang to a small guitar,
"O lovely Pussy! O Pussy, my love,
What a beautiful Pussy you are, you are, you are,
What a beautiful Pussy you are."
Pussy said to the Owl, "You elegant fowl,
How charmingly sweet you sing.
O let us be married, too long we have tarried;
But what shall we do for a ring?"
They sailed away, for a year and a day,
To the land where the Bong-tree grows,
And there in a wood a Piggy-wig stood
With a ring at the end of his nose, his nose, his nose,
With a ring at the end of his nose.
"Dear Pig, are you willing to sell for one shilling your ring?"
Said the Piggy, "I will."
So they took it away, and were married next day
By the Turkey who lives on the hill.
They dined on mince, and slices of quince,
Which they ate with a runcible spoon.
And hand in hand, on the edge of the sand,
They danced by the light of the moon, the moon, the moon,
They danced by the light of the moon.

5. Complete these sentences about the poem by filling in one word.
   a. The owl went sailing with a ______________________
   b. Their boat was ______________________
   c. They sailed for a year and a ______________________
   d. They bought a wedding ring from a ______________________
   e. After their wedding they ate ______________________
   f. They danced by the light of the ______________________

Adjectives

Adjectives tell you more about nouns. For example, in the poem, the owl and the pussycat have a beautiful pea-green boat.

Some adjectives tell you how much of something there is. These are called adjectives of quantity. For example, hundreds of seagulls or many moons. If you ask how much or how many, the answer will be an adjective of quantity.

6. Poetry often makes use of adjectives (sometimes with alliteration) to create a mental picture of something. Use at least three adjectives to describe each item below in a creative and poetic way.

a long, beat-up leather boot

7. Write an adjective of quantity to answer these questions based on the poem on page 15.
   a. How much honey did they have? ______________
   b. How much money did they have? ______________
   c. How many pounds did they use to wrap things up? ______________
   d. How many shillings did they pay for their ring? ______________
   e. How many guests attended their wedding? ______________

4 Writing poetry

Before you begin

- Work with a partner. Read these four lines from a poem carefully. What effect has the poet tried to create?

  One wobbly wheel
  Two trains turning
  Three thumping thingamajigs
  Four flaming fires flashing

- Make up four more lines of your own.

  Five ____________________
  Six ____________________
  Seven ____________________
  Eight ____________________

1. Mrs Playfair asked her class what advice they would give people who want to write a poem. Read what the pupils said.

2. Work with your partner. Use the advice that the children gave Mrs Playfair on page 17 to develop a ten-point checklist for writing and editing your own poem.

Ten-point checklist for writing and editing your own poems

1. ______________________________

2. ______________________________

3. ______________________________

4. ______________________________

5. ______________________________

6. ______________________________

7. ______________________________

8. ______________________________

9. ______________________________

10. ______________________________

Syllables

A syllable is a part of a word that contains a single vowel sound. For example:

- cat has one syllable: cat
- mutton has two syllables: mut/ton
- telephone has three syllables: tel/e/phone
- caterpillar has four syllables: cat/er/pil/lar

Syllables give the structure in some types of poetry.

3. Draw lines to break these words into syllables. Write how many syllables each word has.

umbrella ____	piano ____	elephant ____	crunchy ____
hippopotamus ____	treasure ____	damp ____	computer ____
syllable ____	impossible ____	diamond ____	ocean ____

4. Read these short poems.
   a. Write the number of syllables in each line in the boxes.
   b. Write a sentence describing the pattern in each poem.

The cloud

Big ☐
Flimsy ☐
Weightless ball ☐
Slowly expands ☐
As it shuffles past ☐

______

______

Holidays

The last bell has rung ☐
Desk lids dropping ☐
Kids laughter ☐
Rushing ☐
Out ☐

______

______

5. Write your own syllable poems. Use the number of syllables shown in the box for each line.

Syllable poems

When you write a syllable poem, you have to think carefully about the topic and choose your words carefully to paint a picture that appeals to the reader.

The dentist

______ 1
______ 2
______ 2
______ 5
______ 2
______ 2

The ocean

______ 1
______ 2
______ 3
______ 4
______ 5
______ 6

Haiku

A haiku is a Japanese form of verse that contains exactly seventeen syllables. The verse is arranged in three lines with the syllable pattern 5:7:5. Here is a haiku about a hummingbird.

Writing a haiku is challenging because you need to choose your words carefully and stick to the strict rules.

Hummingbird

At the hibiscus
Rainbow wings flutter wildly
While a beak dives in

6. Ricardo has drafted three haiku, but he has not quite got the syllables correct.
   a. Read the three haiku.
   b. Find the line with the incorrect number of syllables.
   c. Rewrite the line so that it has the correct number of syllables.
   d. Read your completed haiku to a partner.

Beach glass

Broken glass on the sand ______________________
Glistening in the midday sun ______________________
Like broken jewels ______________________

Carnival

Five jumblies on stilts ______________________
Clip, clip, clop along they come ______________________
Towering ghosts ______________________

Piano

Hands stepping stiffly ______________________
Across the zebra stripes ______________________
Music marches out ______________________

7. Write a haiku of your own. Choose one of the following topics.

kitten | seagull | school bell | lunch

____
____
____
____

Cinquains

A cinquain is a five-line poem written in a particular pattern.
Line 1 names the subject of the poem using only one word.
Line 2 tells you more about the subject using only two words.
Line 3 describes an action in three words, they are usually words ending in -ing.
Line 4 expresses an opinion or feeling in four words.
Line 5 is one word that can either be a synonym for the subject or a word that sums up the previous four lines.

8. Read this cinquain carefully.

Dentist
Masked madman
Drilling, scraping, pulling
I'm a shivering wreck
Torturer

a. What is the subject of the poem? __________
b. What synonym is used for the subject later in the poem? __________
c. What actions are carried out? __________
d. What feeling is expressed? __________

9. Complete these two cinquains using the rules.

Storm
Angry __________
Breaking, __________
Scary __________
____

Birthday
Happy __________
Singing __________
We __________
Party

10. Which of the completed cinquains do you like the best? Why?

5 Playing ball

Before you begin

- Look at these pictures of three different ball games.
  - Which game is being played in each picture? How do you know this?
  - Which famous sports stars do you know who play these games? Tell your partner their names and which game they play.

1. Read this information about the history of football on your own.

The history of football

Football (or soccer, as it is known in some countries) is a very old game. Historians have found evidence that the ancient Greeks, Romans, Egyptians, Chinese and Japanese played a ball game similar to football thousands of years ago. In China, the ball was made of leather and stuffed with feathers.

Modern football was born in England, where it started as a wild and sometimes violent game often played between whole villages of people. There were no real rules and you could do anything to get the ball into the opponent's net except "murder or manslaughter".

In the 1800s the game became more organised and formal. In 1863, the rules of the game were standardised. At this time football split from another game called rugby football, with the rule that you cannot use your hands in football at all unless you are the goalkeeper. Once the rules were agreed on, it took another nine years for the size and weight of the ball to become standardised.

Football was first played at schools and universities. The Football Association (FA) organised the first football tournament in 1871. Today, millions of people follow the British FA Cup tournament.

The first "international" game of football was played in 1872 between Scotland and England. By 1885, the FA accepted the idea of professional football players and in 1888 it set up a regular and organised league.

 SKILLS: Discuss different ball games. Read an information text.

For the rest of the 1800s, the game spread to other countries through traders, sailors and soldiers. Football became very popular in Europe and South America. In 1904, the Fédération Internationale de Football Association (FIFA) was founded in Paris, France, with seven members. By 1921 FIFA had grown to 21 members, by 1925 it had 35 and by 1930, when the first Football World Cup competition was held, it had 41 members. Today, FIFA is the governing body of the sport worldwide and it organises the World Cup competitions that are hosted by different countries every four years.

The closing ceremony at the 2010 FIFA World Cup in South Africa.

2. The following statements about the history of football are all false. Rewrite them to make them true.
   a. The ancient Chinese played football with a wooden ball.
   b. The rules of modern football were set up by FIFA.
   c. The FA Cup tournament is a worldwide competition held every four years.
   d. The first Football World Cup was played in 1896.
   e. Professional football teams can decide what the size and weight of the ball should be.
   f. In football, players are allowed to touch the ball with their hands.

3. Complete this football timeline by adding the dates at which different events happened.

Timelines
A timeline is a diagram that shows the order in which events happened and when they happened.

1. Modern football begins in England ______
2. First rules of football agreed ______
3. Size and weight of ball agreed ______
4. First FA Cup tournament organised ______
5. First international football match ______
6. FIFA founded in Paris ______
7. First Football World Cup ______

Homonyms
Homonyms are words that have the same spelling and sound, but different meanings. For example:
Save means "put money in the bank" in everyday life.
Save also means "stop the ball going into the goal" in football.

4. Here are some words used to talk about different actions in football.
   a. Match each word to its meaning.

score	try to get a goal but fail
pass	score the same number of goals as the other team
shoot	kick the ball to another player
head	kick the ball into the goal
miss	hit the ball with your head
draw	control the ball with your feet and move it around
dribble	try to kick the ball into the goal

   b. Work with your partner. What other meanings do these words have?

score ______
pass ______
shoot ______
head ______
miss ______
draw ______
dribble ______

5. Read this newspaper article carefully with your partner.

The highest-paid player in the world

Sarah Melville

Its official! Lionel Messi (photo on right) was the highest-paid footballer in the world during 2011. The Barcelona player, who has twice won the world footballer of the year award, earned a staggering US$44 million in salaries and promotional deals. That's around $850 000 per week.

Second place in the high-earner stakes goes to Real Madrid's Cristiano Ronaldo on US$34 million and third goes to Manchester United's Wayne Rooney on US$29 million.

The English Premier League seems to offer the most money, with 7 of the 20 top-earning players in 2011 being in that league.

6. Answer these questions about the article.
   a. Who wrote the article?
   b. Who was the world's highest-paid footballer in 2011?
   c. Which club did he play for?
   d. Which player earned the third highest amount?
   e. How much did Cristiano Ronaldo earn in 2011?
   f. How many of the top 20 highest-paid players play in England?

7. Rachel's grandfather read this article and he was outraged. He says that in his opinion it is ridiculous and immoral to pay people so much money for playing a game they love, and that sport should be played for fun and not money. Do you agree or disagree with his opinion? Have a discussion in your group. Give reasons for your opinions.

8. Many highly paid professional footballers come from underprivileged backgrounds. Many of them work with charities and non-profit organisations to develop the sport and help people who are less fortunate. Read this information from the website of the 1GOAL Campaign, which was launched during the 2010 FIFA World Cup.

THE 1GOAL CAMPAIGN

Today, 67 million children in the world are denied the chance to go to school. These children could be the next generation's leaders, sports stars, doctors and teachers. But they face a lifelong struggle against poverty.

It doesn't have to be this way. Since 2000, 40 million more children are in school. Education beats poverty – and gives people the tools to help themselves.

1GOAL is a campaign seizing the power of football to get all children into school and learning. Raising our voices all over the world we believe that, together, we can make education a reality for the millions of boys and girls who remain out of school.

"This is our chance to show not just out-of-school children, but our own children, that when we make a promise, we keep it. With your help, we could have billions of fans cheering not just for their teams, but for one team: 1GOAL. This is our moment to shine; we can bring millions of children in from the shadows of ignorance, and light up their lives with the legacy of education." ~ Her Majesty Queen Rania Al-Abdullah, co-founder and global co-chair, 1GOAL

You can help make education for all a reality.

1GOAL brings together footballers, fans, charities, corporations and individuals to lobby and achieve our ambitious aim of education for everyone. By joining the 1GOAL team, you can strengthen the campaign's voice and give us the best possible chance of success.

9. Answer these questions about the 1GOAL Campaign.
   a. What does the 1GOAL Campaign aim to do?
   b. Why is this important?
   c. What can famous football players do to help meet the aims of the 1GOAL Campaign? Make a list of three things.

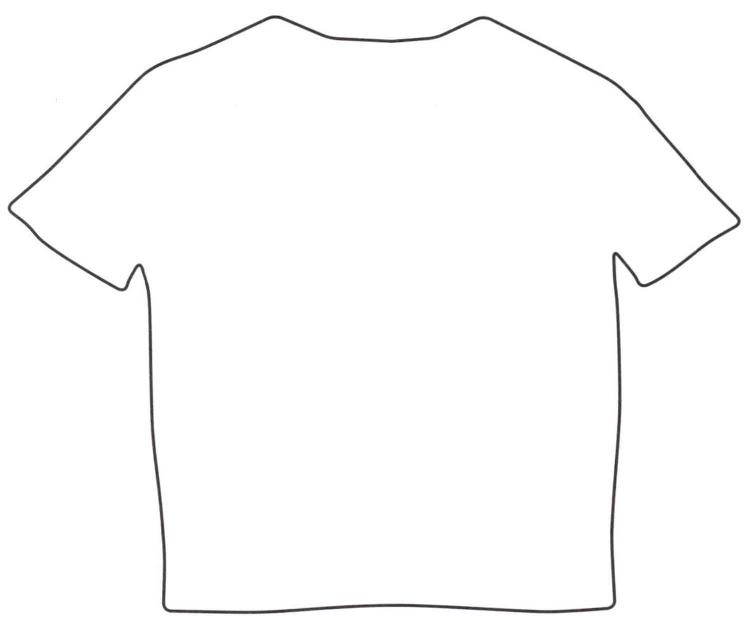

10. Design a T-shirt logo and a short slogan to help raise awareness of the work done by the 1GOAL Campaign.

 SKILLS: Read website information. Answer questions. Design a logo and write a slogan.

11. Read this text about women's football.

Women at the Football World Cup

Today, women's football is growing in popularity, but it still falls well behind men's football. The Women's World Cup also takes place every four years, one year later than the men's competition.

The first Women's World Cup took place in China in 1991 (a full 61 years after the first men's tournament). Only 16 countries competed, compared with 32 countries in the men's competition.

Winners

1991 – USA
1995 – Norway
1999 – USA
2003 – Germany
2007 – Germany
2011 – Japan

Japan's Kumagai scores the winn ng penalty at the 2011 Women's World Cup final in Frankfurt.

At the 2011 Women's World Cup in Germany, 18 countries took part. Japan was the surprise winner, beating two-times champions, the USA, in a penalty shoot-out to win the final match and walk off with the trophy.

The 2015 Women's World Cup will take place in Canada.

12. Here are the answers to six questions about the Women's World Cup. For each answer, write down what question you think was asked.

a. Question: ______
   Answer: 1991
b. Question: ______
   Answer: China
c. Question: ______
   Answer: The USA and Germany
d. Question: ______
   Answer: Japan
e. Question: ______
   Answer: By a penalty shoot-out.
f. Question: ______
   Answer: Canada

6 Cricket

Before you begin

- Here are three cartoons based on cricket sayings.
  - What does each saying actually mean?
  - How are the cartoons meant to be funny?

Googly

Out for a duck

A dolly catch

1. In a television programme called "West Indian Cricket Legends", the following players were named as legends: George Headley, Sir Garfield Sobers, Sir Viv Richards, Sir Frank Worrell and Brian Lara.
   a. Read the information about each player on your own.

George Alphonso Headley (1909–1983)
Born in Panama and raised in Jamaica
Considered one of the best batsmen to play for West Indies (WI) and one of the greatest cricketers ever. Batted at number 3 and scored over 2000 runs in test cricket. Captained the WI team in 1948 against England. When he retired he was chosen to coach the Jamaican team. His son Ron and his grandson Dean both became test cricketers.

Sir Garfield St Auburn Sobers (Garry) (born 1936)
From Bridgetown, Barbados
Considered the best ever all-rounder in cricket, Sir Garry held the world individual record for the highest test innings with 365 not out until this record was beaten by Brian Lara in 1994.

Sir Garry was the first player to score six sixes in an over in first-class cricket. He played for the West Indies 93 times, 39 of these as captain.

Sir Isaac Vivian Alexander Richards (Viv) (born 1952)
From St John's, Antigua
Sir Viv Richards captained the WI team from 1986–1991 and was the only captain under whom the West Indies never lost a series. Known for scoring runs, he holds the record for the highest number of runs scored in test cricket in one year (1710 runs during 1976). Now retired, he was voted one of the top five cricketers of the century in 2000.

Sir Frank Mortimer Maglinne Worrell (Tae) (1924–1967)
Born in Barbados, relocated to Jamaica
Sir Frank became famous in the 1950s as the first black captain of the WI team. He is the only batsman to have been involved in two 500-run partnerships in first-class cricket. When he retired from cricket he became a senator and a warden at the University of the West Indies. One of the halls of residence at Cave Hill Campus in Barbados is named after him. The Frank Worrell trophy for winners of the test series between the West Indies and Australia is also named after him.

The honourable Brian Charles Lara (born 1969)
From Port of Spain, Trinidad
Brian Lara became well known as the captain of the West Indies team. In 1994, he broke the world individual batting record (previously held by Sir Garfield Sobers) by scoring 375 runs against England. Later that year he scored an unbeaten 501 in first-class cricket. He remains the only batsman to have scored a century, a double century, a triple century, a quadruple century and a quintuple century over the course of his career. He also scored 28 runs in one over against South Africa in 2003.

b. Choose one modern cricket player that you consider to be a legend. Add a photograph or draw a picture of the player you have chosen in the frame below. Then complete the information about this player.

Name: ______________________ Date of birth: ______________________
From: ____
Achievements: ______________________________________
____
____
____
____
____
____

2. Shawn did a survey among 30 of his classmates to find out what type of cricket they liked best. He showed his results in a pie chart. Study the pie chart and then answer the questions.

Which type of cricket do you prefer?

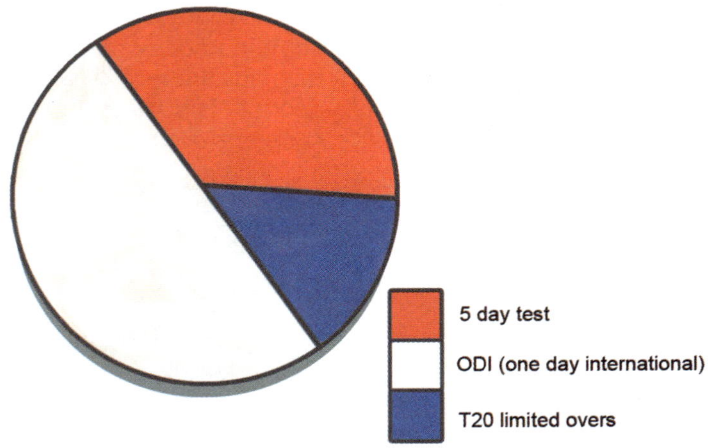

   a. How many children did he ask? ______________________

   b. What question do you think he asked them? ______________________

   c. What fraction of the children like ODI cricket best? ______________________

   d. Which is more popular, 5 day tests or T20 limited overs cricket? ______________________

   e. Which type of cricket do you like best? Why? ______________________

3. Carry out your own survey among your friends to find out which type of cricket they prefer.

   a. Use this tally table to record your results.

Type of cricket	Tally	Total
5 day test		
ODI		
T20 limited overs		

   b. Use the results of your survey to complete this pie chart.

Type of cricket preferred by my friends

Key

☐ 5 day test
☐ ODI
☐ T20 limited overs

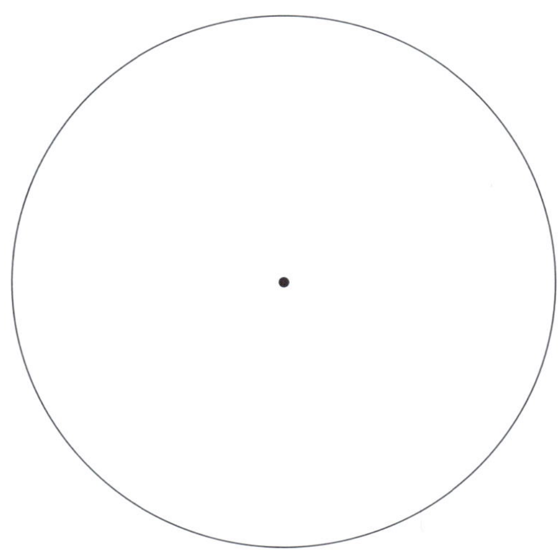

   c. Write two sentences to summarise what your graph shows.

____

____

 SKILLS: Interpret a pie chart. Conduct a survey. Complete a tally table and a pie chart. Write a summary.

Facts, opinions and exaggerations

A fact is something that is true. For example: Sir Viv Richards was born in Antigua.

An opinion is something that you think. An opinion may be true, but it may not be true. For example: I think Brian Lara was the best captain ever.

An exaggeration is a statement that makes something appear bigger, smaller, better or worse than it actually is. For example: Reports that the captain threw his gloves at the manager after losing the match are exaggerated. He simply took off the gloves and dropped them onto the floor.

4. Read this letter to a newspaper after a recent poor performance by a cricket team.

Dear Editor

On Saturday our team lost by 150 runs. Is it just me, or was that game the worst in the history of cricket? As a long-time cricket supporter, I have to express my extreme disappointment at the losing performance of our team. They need to go back to the drawing board and learn how to play, both the game, and as a team. I think they played worse than novices.

I also think we need to educate our cricket-watching public. There were 4 500 people at the game, according to the ticket sales. I'd estimate that more than three-quarters of them were more concerned with their food and drinks and their mobile phones than they were with the actual game. I swear I saw some people who slept through the entire thing.

This team is a disgrace. Not only did they play poorly, they bent the rules and looked shoddy doing it. It appeared to me that there was quite a lot of sledging and insult trading and more than one incident of ball tampering.

Of course, the umpire did nothing at all to help the situation. A more inept performance is difficult to imagine.

Yours in disappointment
Mr James Purefoy

a. Use blue to underline two facts in this letter.
b. Use red to underline two opinions in this letter.
c. Find one exaggeration. Circle it.

5. Answer these questions about the letter on page 31.
   a. Was the writer pleased with the performance of the team? How do you know this?

   ____

   b. Is the letter fair? Give a reason for your answer.

   ____

   c. What is the tone of the person writing the letter? How do you know this?

   ____

   d. How do you think each of these people might feel if they read this letter.
   - The team captain: ______________________________
   - A supporter who was at the match: ______________________________
   - The umpire: ______________________________
   - A player from the winning team: ______________________________

6. Read this information about the 2015 Cricket World Cup.

The 2015 Cricket World Cup

The International Cricket Council (ICC) has confirmed that the 2015 World Cup will comprise the ten current full members of the ICC plus four additional teams which will be picked during the 2013 ICC World Cup Qualifier.

The ten current members are:

India	Sri Lanka
Pakistan	New Zealand
South Africa	Australia
England	West Indies
Bangladesh	Zimbabwe

Other teams who could qualify in 2013 are:

Afghanistan	Scotland
Canada	Hong Kong
Ireland	Namibia
Kenya	Papua New Guinea
Netherlands	United Arab Emirates

7. Look at this map and the information on page 32 and answer the questions.

a. Find each country mentioned on page 32 on a world map. Now draw a line from each flag to where the country would be on this map.

b. The West Indies are a team, not a country. How can you show where the West Indies are on the map?

____

c. Choose one country's flag. Write a clear description of the flag here.

Name of country: ______________________________

Description of flag: ____________________________

____

____

____

____

SKILLS: Interpret a map and information text. Write a description.

7 Track and field

Before you begin

- Look at these pictures carefully.
  - Write the name of each event shown.
  - Circle the track events.
  - Underline the field events.

1. Here are some track and field events. Rewrite them in alphabetical order.

javelin | hurdles | marathon | high jump | triple jump

discus | pole vault | relay | shot-put | sprint

 SKILLS: Interpret pictures. Categorise information. List words in alphabetical order.

2. Read these definitions carefully. Find a word from your alphabetical list on page 34 to match each definition. Write the word in the space provided.

______________________: an event in which the athlete tries to throw a long stick with a pointed end a long distance

______________________: a short, fast race, usually run over 100 m or 200 m

______________________: a slow-paced race run over a long distance

______________________: a competition in which athletes jump over a bar to see who can jump the highest

______________________: a race in which the athletes have to run and jump over small barriers

______________________: a competition in which the athlete hops, steps and then does a jump to land with both feet in a sand pit

______________________: an event in which athletes throw a flat, round disc as far as they can

______________________: a team race in which a baton is passed from one runner to the next

______________________: a jumping competition in which the athlete uses a long stick to get greater height

______________________: an event in which athletes throw a heavy metal ball as far as they can

3. Skim read this text about track events on your own. Then answer the questions on page 36.

Athletics: Track events

Track events take place on a running track. Athletics tracks are oval, with a field in the centre. Most tracks are 400 m long. The track itself is divided up into lanes, which are marked with lines so the athletes know which lane is theirs. The surface of the track can be grass, rubberised material or a special kind of tar.

Sprints

Races over short distances (100 m, 200 m and 400 m) are called sprints. Each sprinter starts in a separate lane and they have to stay in their own lane for the whole race. Most professional athletes start the race with their feet in blocks and their hands on the track. When the starting gun is fired, they push out of the blocks and run as fast as they can to the finish line.

Usain Bolt of Jamaica is currently the world record holder for the 100 m and 200 m sprint.

The 2011 Jamaican relay team

Relay races

A relay team consists of four runners who run as a team. They take turns to run a certain distance carrying a baton. At the end of the distance, the runner passes the baton to his or her team mate and that person runs the next part of the race. Relay races are often the highlight of an athletics meeting. Nesta Carter, Michael Frater, Yohan Blake and Usain Bolt set a new world record for the 4 × 100 m relay at the 2011 IAAF World Athletics Championships.

Middle- to long-distance races

Runners can also compete in 800 m, 1500 m and 3000 m races. There is also a 5000 m and 10000 m event on the track. These races are slower than the sprint, but the athletes need to be fit to keep up their pace for the whole race.

The longest race is the marathon. A standard marathon is 42 km long and it is usually run on roads away from the stadium.

a. What shape is an athletics track?

b. How far will you run if you run once around the track?

c. What is a sprinter?

d. Who holds the world record for the 100 m and 200 m sprint?

e. Which country won the 4 x 100 m relay at the 2011 IAAF World Athletics Championships?

f. What is a middle-distance race?

g. Which running event is not run on the track? Explain why not.

 SKILLS: Skim read an information text. Answer questions.

Prefixes

A prefix is a set of letters added to the beginning of a word. Most prefixes have a meaning. For example, the prefix tri- means three. It can be added to the word cycle to form the world tricycle which means three-wheeler. It can also be added to the word athlete to make the word triathlete. A triathlete competes in a triathlon, which is a three-event competition including a running race, a cycle race and a swimming race.

4. The prefix deca- means ten. Write down what each of these words means.
   a. decathlon: ____________________
   b. decagon: ____________________
   c. decade: ____________________
   d. decalogue: ____________________
   e. decametre: ____________________

5. Find and circle ten words related to track and field events in this wordsearch.

S	P	R	I	N	T	E	R	X	B	J
Q	R	E	S	A	Z	X	C	V	A	X
D	L	L	A	N	E	G	U	O	T	N
I	M	A	R	A	T	H	O	N	O	W
S	P	Y	E	E	S	U	I	U	N	E
C	W	A	U	V	T	R	A	C	K	Z
U	R	E	C	O	R	D	I	L	Z	L
S	O	I	K	A	U	L	M	B	Q	S
Y	F	G	J	A	V	E	L	I	N	P

6. Work with your partner. Take turns to use five words from the wordsearch in sentences to show that you know what they mean.

7. Read the statements in the first column of the table below.
   a. Tick the correct column to show whether each statement is true or false.
   b. Tell your partner why the false statements are false.

Statement	True	False
An athletics track is a 400 m long oval that is divided into lanes.		
The relay is a team event in which runners have to clear small hurdles as they run.		
Middle-distance events are run between 100 m and 400 m.		
The marathon takes about two weeks to complete.		
The longest event run on the track is the 3 000 m race.		
The fastest man in the world is Michael Johnson of the USA.		

8. Here are the world record holders for the sprint races, with their times and the year in which they set their record.

Event	Men			Women		
	Record (in seconds)	Record holder	Year set	Record (in seconds)	Record holder	Year set
100 m	9.58	Usain Bolt (Jamaica)	2009	10.49	Florence Griffith-Joyner (USA)	1988
200 m	19.19	Usain Bolt (Jamaica)	2009	21.34	Florence Griffith-Joyner (USA)	1988
400 m	43.18	Michael Johnson (USA)	1999	47.60	Marita Koch (Germany)	1985

a. Make up five questions that can be answered from the table. Use at least three different question words (who, what, when, how much, how long) in your questions.

b. Exchange questions with a partner and try to answer each other's questions.

 SKILLS: Identify true and false statements. Interpret a table. Write questions. Answer questions.

9. Petula found this completed crossword puzzle on the floor, but the clues were missing. Work with a partner. Write a set of clues that work for this crossword puzzle.

				a M									b L
		1 C	H	A	M	P	I	O	N	c S			A
				R						P			N
				A				2 H	U	R	D	L	E
		3 B	A	T	O	N				I			
				H						N			
				O						T			
4 d T	R	A	I	N					5 e R	E	L	A	Y
R					6 R	U	N	N	E	R			
A									C				
7 C	O	M	P	E	T	I	T	I	O	N			
K									R				
									D				

ACROSS
1. ______
2. ______
3. ______
4. ______
5. ______
6. ______
7. ______

DOWN
a. ______
b. ______
c. ______
d. ______
e. ______

8 Sport at school

Before you begin

- Work on your own. Draw lines from the activities on the left to the terms that relate to them on the right.

- football
- cricket
- tennis
- basketball
- netball
- cycling
- running
- skateboarding
- computer games
- chess
- table tennis
- karate

- ramp
- belt
- goalpost
- bicycle
- racquet
- bowl
- shoot
- joystick
- board
- ball
- hoop
- track
- bat

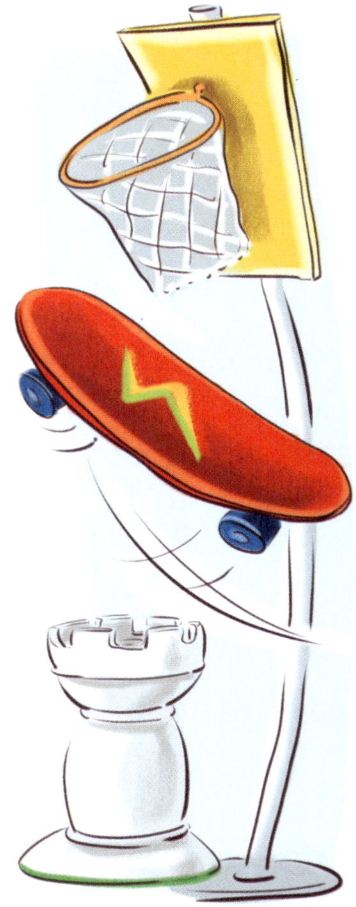

- Compare your answers with a partner. Are they the same?
- Discuss why you could have different answers for this activity.

1. Read the notice on page 41 that a school principal sent out to the parents.

2. a. Make up your own questions about the notice. Start with the question words given.
   b. Then exchange questions with another pupil and answer each other's questions.

Question: When ____

Answer: ____

Question: Where ____

Answer: ____

Question: How ______________________________

Answer: ______________________________

Question: What ______________________________

Answer: ______________________________

Question: Which ______________________________

Answer: ______________________________

Question: Who ______________________________

Answer: ______________________________

MOUNT VIEW PRIMARY SCHOOL

23 January

Dear Parents and Guardians

This is to notify you that this year's interschool athletics meet will be hosted by St Mary's Primary School. The meet will take place from 8.00 a.m. to 1.00 p.m. on Friday, 2 February.

Please note the following arrangements.
Pupils will be transported to the meet by contract buses. Each child must pay $60 for bus fare by Wednesday, 31 January. Any pupils who cannot afford this amount should contact Ms Jones-Hamilton at the school to arrange for assistance in this regard.

The buses will leave school promptly at 7.20 a.m. on Friday, 2 February. Any pupil who arrives later than that will not be transported to the meet and will have to remain at school. Supervision will be provided.

Pupils will be returned to the school by 2.00 p.m. They should make their own arrangements to get home from school.

All pupils who are taking part must complete an entry form and return a signed indemnity form (attached). Pupils who fail to return these forms will not be permitted to take part in any events.

If you have any queries in this regard, please contact Mr Bolt, the sports co-ordinator at the school.

Yours sincerely

Gladys J. Morgan
Principal

3. Imagine you are taking part in the interschool athletics meet. You are a member of the Red House. Design a flag with a short slogan on it to support and encourage your team.

SKILLS: Read a notice. Write and answer questions. Design a flag and write a slogan.

4. After the athletics meet all the sports co-ordinators from the different schools had a meeting to discuss some of the problems that were experienced at the event. They identified the eight problems listed in the table below.
   a. Work with a partner. Read through the problems. Say what you think caused each problem.
   b. How could these problems be avoided in the future? Discuss your ideas and then write the solutions in the table using point-form notes.

Problems	Possible solutions
1. Some buses arrived late, so the meet did not start on time.	
2. Runners could not hear the announcements, so many of them did not arrive for their events when called.	
3. The lines on the track were not clearly marked, so many runners ran out of their lanes and were disqualified.	
4. Children moved around and did not stay with their school groups on the stands.	
5. The first-aid tent was unable to cope with all the incidents and injuries and it ran out of ice-packs before 10.00 a.m.	
6. Children from some schools booed participants during certain events and generally behaved in an unruly manner.	
7. Participants and spectators had to use one public bathroom and this soon got overcrowded and dirty.	
8. There was an immense amount of litter left lying around after the event (including lots of broken glass).	

 SKILLS: Read, interpret and find solutions for problems.

5. The sports co-ordinators agreed that many of the problems could have been avoided or prevented if there had been a clear set of rules for everyone involved in the event. Work in small groups. Imagine that you are a committee that was set up to draft rules for future athletics meets.
   a. Discuss which things participants must do. Choose four things that you think are the most important.
   b. Discuss which things participants may not do. Choose four things that you think are the most important.
   c. Write your ideas as a set of rules in the table below.

Participants must:	**Participants may not:**
1.	1.
2.	2.
3.	3.
4.	4.

6. At the next athletics meet everyone obeyed the rules and the event went very well. Imagine you are a parent who attended the first meet and found it disgraceful. You have just attended the recent meet and you were very impressed. Write a positive letter to the principal of your child's school to tell her about your experience.

12 Electric Avenue
Kingston
7 February

Dear Mrs Morgan

Yours sincerely

Sam Johnson

9 Climates around the world

Before you begin

- Discuss these questions in your group.
  - How would you describe the climate in Jamaica?
  - What types of plants and animals are suited to the climate in Jamaica?
  - What types of plants and animals are not well suited to the climate in Jamaica? Why not?
  - If you had to choose between living in a hot place or a cold place, which would you choose? Why?

1. Work with a partner. Study the graph and read the labels carefully to learn how to make sense of climate graphs.

Climate graph for London

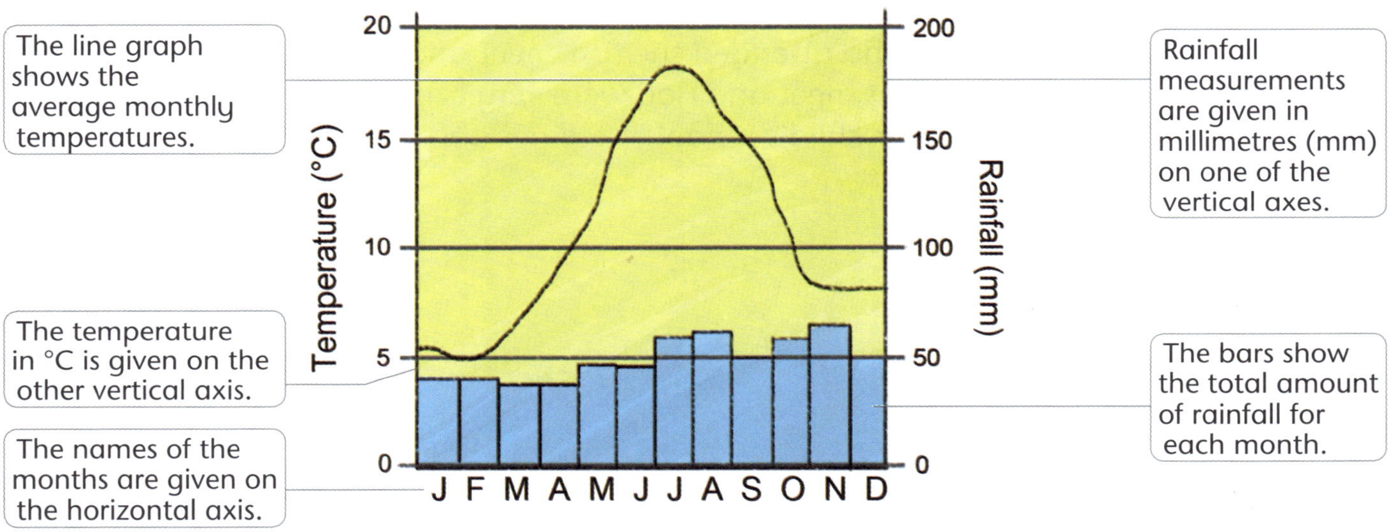

2. Answer these questions about the climate graph for London.
   a. Which month is the warmest? What is the average temperature in that month?

   ____

   b. Which two months have the lowest rainfall? How many millimetres of rain fall during these two months?

   ____

   c. Which three months of the year are the coldest in London?

   ____

   d. How does the climate in London differ from the climate in Jamaica?

   ____

 SKILLS: Discuss questions. Read, interpret and answer questions about a climate graph.

3. In the box below are some words and phrases that are often used to talk about temperature and rainfall in different places.
   a. Discuss the words with a partner and make sure you understand them all.

Temperature	**Rainfall**
mild to hot	arid (dry)
cold	heavy
hot	moderate to heavy
cool to mild	light to moderate
very hot	very heavy
freezing	

   b. Complete the two tables below by writing the phrases that are used to talk about temperature and rainfall in the correct places.

Temperature	Phrases used to describe temperature
> 30 °C	
20–30 °C	
15–20 °C	
10–15 °C	
0–10 °C	
< 0 °C	

Rainfall (per annum)	Phrases used to describe rainfall
> 1 500 mm	
1 000–1 500 mm	
750–1 000 mm	
250–750 mm	
< 250 mm	

   c. Use the words above (and others you may know) to write a short description of the climate in London during summer and winter. Use the graph on page 44 to find the information you need.
   - Summers in London are: ______
   - Winters in London are: ______

4. a. Study this climate graph for Cairo, Egypt, carefully.
   b. Circle the descriptions that apply to the climate in Cairo.

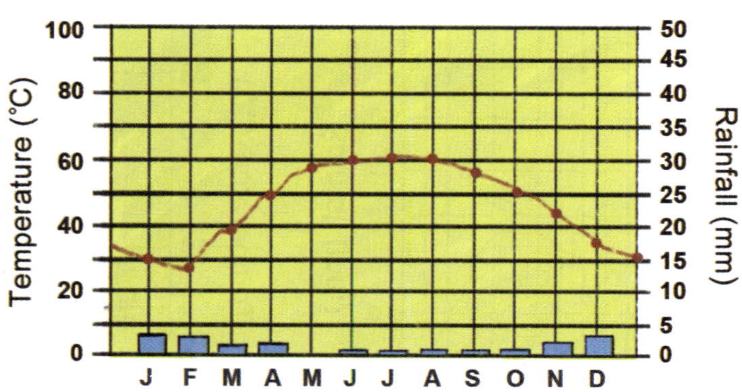

hot all year | cool winters | light to moderate rainfall | warm summers | very light rain | arid | freezing winters

5. There are three main climate regions in the world. The map below shows you where each region is found. The graphs show you the climate conditions in each region.
   a. Spend some time reading and talking about the map and the graphs with your partner.
   b. Ask each other questions to make sure you can read and make sense of the map and the graphs. Name some countries found in each region shown on the map.

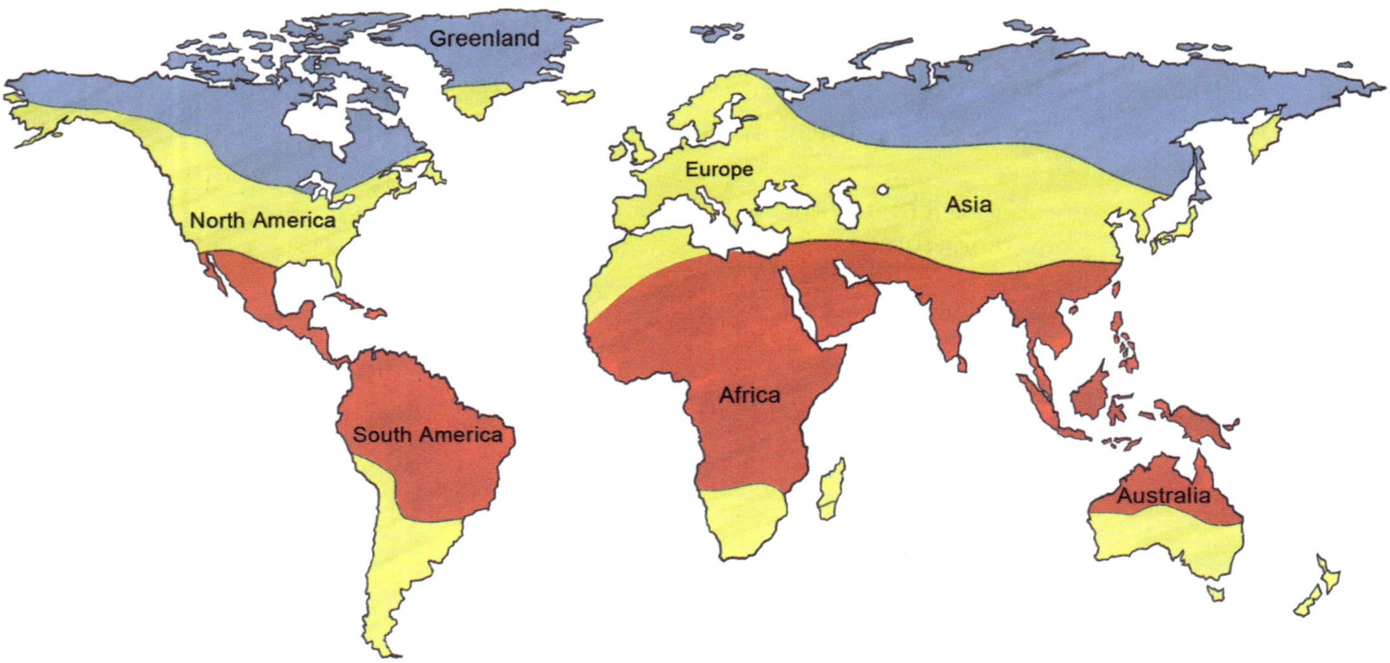

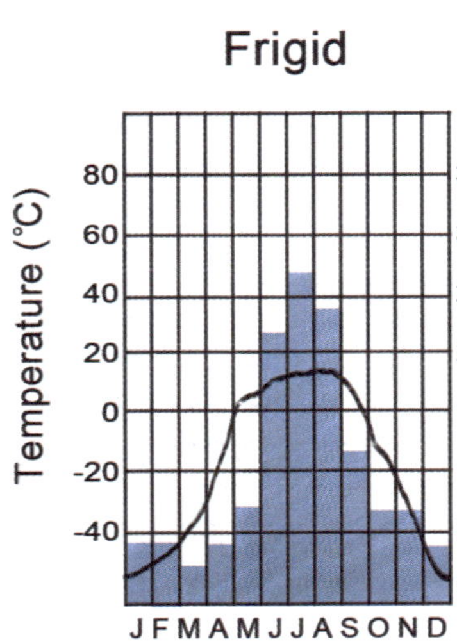

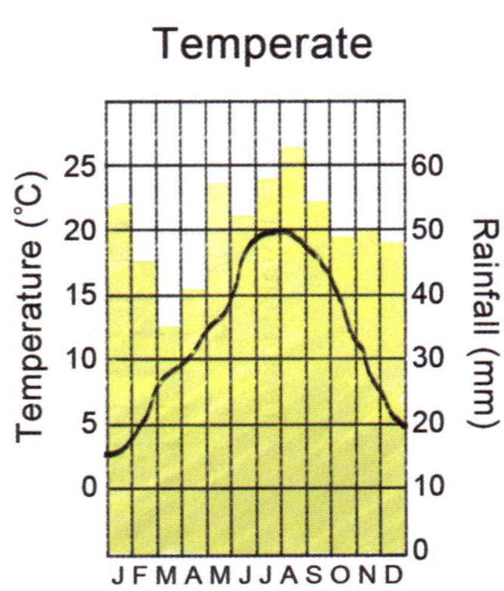

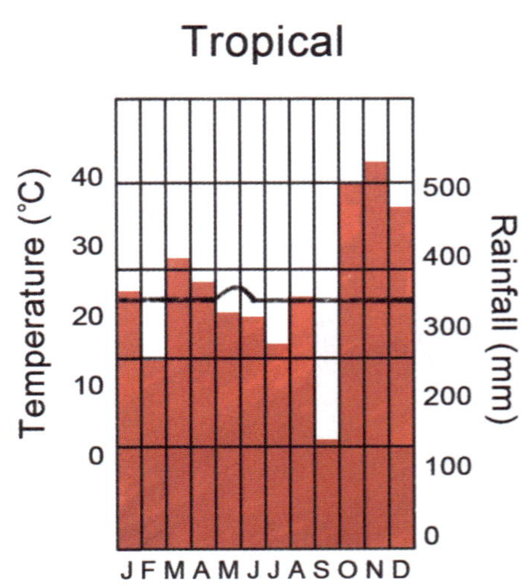

6. Use the phrases you have learnt and find information from the map and the graphs to complete this table.

	Frigid region	Temperate region	Tropical region
Three examples of countries in this region			
Rainfall patterns in this region			
Summer temperature conditions			
Winter temperature conditions			
General description of the climate of this region			

10 Life in the tropics

Before you begin

- Work with your partner. Identify each of these animals and write their names in the space provided.

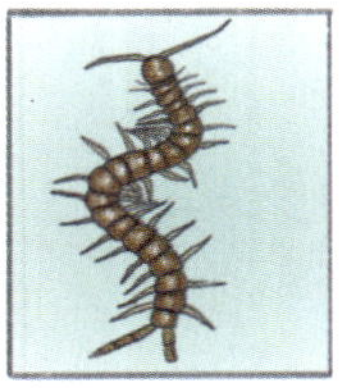       

- Underline the names of the animals you have seen in real life.
- All of these animals, except for one, are found in tropical forests. Which animal does not belong to the group? Where does this animal live?

1. Look at the animals in the pictures above. Read these fact files.
   a. Which animal is being described? Write the name of the animal as a heading.
   b. Add one more fact to each fact file.

Animal's name: ______	**Another interesting fact**
These fruit-eaters like to climb trees. They use their tails and arms to swing from branch to branch. They are messy eaters and they drop lots of fruit on the ground. This helps the seeds to spread and allows new fruit trees to grow.	

Animal's name: ______	**Another interesting fact**
These many-legged creatures are mostly nocturnal. They feed on dead animal matter found on the forest floor.	

Animal's name: ______	**Another interesting fact**
These flying animals are actually mammals. They hang upside down to sleep. They feed on plant nectar and fruits that give off a musty smell that attracts them.	

 SKILLS: Identify animals. Read fact files. Write facts.

Animal's name: ______________________	Another interesting fact
The damp, warm conditions in the forest are ideal for these slimy animals. They live in shallow pools or in the water that collects in plants. They eat algae and small insects. Many of them are brightly coloured and very poisonous.	

Animal's name: ______________________	Another interesting fact
This is a large bird with a long, strong beak that it uses to dig into the bark of trees to find insects and other food.	

Animal's name: ______________________	Another interesting fact
These birds are very colourful. They feed on fruits and nuts. Their beaks are strong and sharp enough to crack open nuts to eat them.	

Animal's name: ______________________	Another interesting fact
These animals are reptiles. They feed on small animals, which they grab and crush to death. They can grow to over 5 metres in length.	

c. Write your own fact file about polar bears.

Animal's name: ______________________	Another interesting fact

2. The wetter parts of the tropical region are home to the world's rainforests.
   a. Study the diagram and the photographs carefully to learn more about the types of vegetation found in tropical rainforests.

   b. Read the statements. Tick whether they are true or false.

Statement	True	False
Rainforests contain many different trees.		
Most trees in the rainforest grow at heights of 100 m.		
The tops of trees form a dense canopy at heights of between 25 m and 35 m.		
The floor of the rainforest is covered with dead and decaying matter.		
Most plants in the rainforest have large green leaves.		

 SKILLS: Read and interpret a diagram and photographs. Categorise statements as true or false.

3. The world's rainforests are being chopped down and destroyed faster than ever before. Many countries have now passed laws to protect their rainforests and to stop them from being destroyed for living space, roads, farm land and wood.

   A reporter from a Jamaican newspaper interviewed Dr Ali, an environmental scientist at UWI, to find out more about this issue.

   a. Read the interview carefully.

Ms Morrison: Is it true that the rainforests could disappear in our lifetime if they continue to be destroyed at the present rate?

Dr Ali: Yes, sadly this is the case. If we continue to destroy these precious natural resources at the same rate, half will be gone by 2025 and all will be lost by 2060. Rainforests used to cover 14% of the world's surface; now they only cover about 5%. The greed for resources continues to rise and as a result, governments and private companies continue to plunder the rainforests.

Ms Morrison: What resources do people get from tropical rainforests?

Dr Ali: One hectare of forest may contain over 750 types of trees and 1 500 species of higher plants. These provide many different products, including timber, nuts, fruit, rubber, cane, cosmetics and medicines.

Ms Morrison: Is that the only reason why forests are being cut down?

Dr Ali: No. Many of the forests are cut down so that the land can be used to farm crops or raise cattle. The companies who remove wood from the forests build roads and destroy many trees in the process. Mining and land clearing to make space for houses also add to the problem.

Ms Morrison: Why is this problem so serious?

Dr Ali: The rainforests protect the soil and keep the climate stable in these areas. Without the forests there is likely to be climate change that will be felt across the world. The rainforests can also be viewed as the Earth's lungs – they produce oxygen and give off water vapour. When the forests are destroyed, the water cycle becomes disrupted and rainfall patterns are affected. In addition, rainforests are home to millions of animal species. Destroying the forests forces these animals to move or they may become extinct.

Ms Morrison: That sounds awful. Is there anything that can be done to prevent the destruction of the rainforests?

Dr Ali: Yes. In some places, national parks have been established to protect the forests. Countries such as Cameroon in West Africa and Malaysia in South-East Asia have set up national parks where plants and animals are protected. In Colombia in South America, the government has given the forests to local people to care for and conserve. In the Caribbean, many tourism and other organisations are part of a project to protect both reefs and rainforests. Ecotourism activities play an important role in this. However, each year, large areas of forest are still destroyed and we all have to act quickly and take the threats seriously to make sure the rainforests survive.

Ms Morrison: Thank you so much for your time and for this valuable information, Dr Ali. Good luck with your research and the good work you do in this area.

b. Read the interview again aloud with a partner. One of you should play the role of the interviewer, Ms Morrison, the other should play the role of Dr Ali.

c. Make a list of five ways in which people use the resources of the rainforests.

d. How will the destruction of rainforests affect both people and animals?

e. Write a short paragraph explaining what you think could be done to conserve rainforests in the Caribbean.

 SKILLS: Read an interview. Compile a list. Answer questions. Write an explanatory paragraph.

4. Read this review of Lynne Cherry's book *The Great Kapok Tree: A Tale of the Amazon Rain Forest*. Then discuss the questions with your partner.

The Great Kapok Tree

Lynne Cherry is an exceptional writer and artist. She personally visited the Amazon rainforest to make sketches and get inspiration for this marvellous picture story. The book stresses the importance of saving the rainforests without sounding dull, or lecturing to us.

The story is a simple one. A man who is sent to cut down a massive kapok tree gets tired and takes a nap. As he sleeps, snakes, butterflies, a jaguar and a sloth that all live in the forest surround him. They take turns to whisper in his ear and tell him about the horrible consequences of living in a world without forests. Finally an Indian child joins them and also whispers in the man's ear. When the man wakes up, he sees all the creatures around him and he has to make a decision about what to do. He decides to put down his axe and walk away.

Enjoyed by millions of children worldwide and translated into several languages, this book is a well-written and beautifully illustrated gem that will add to any reader's collection.

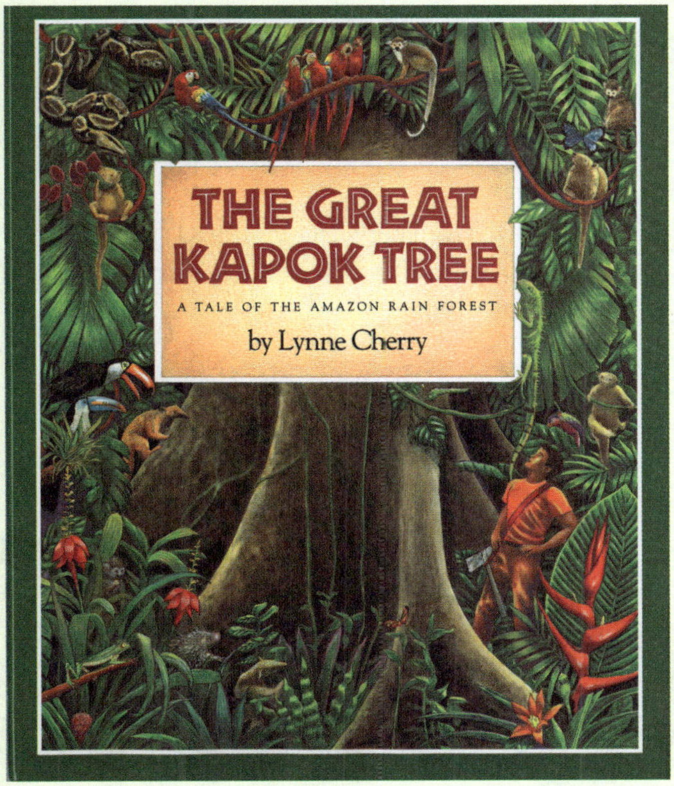

a. Who wrote the book? Who illustrated it?
b. Did the reviewer like the book? How do you know this?
c. Does the review make you want to read the book? Why or why not?
d. Imagine you are one of the forest animals in the story. Which animal would you be? What do you think you would whisper in the man's ear?
e. What do you think the Indian child said to the man?
f. Why do you think the man decided to put down his axe and leave the rainforest alone?

11 Life in the temperate regions

Before you begin

- Work on your own. Which of these countries are in the temperate regions? Circle them.

Japan | Indonesia | Brazil | India | United Kingdom | Jamaica | France | New Zealand | Pakistan | Ghana | Iceland | Norway

- Check your answers by looking in an atlas. Tick the countries that are correct.
- What is the climate like during winter in the temperate regions? Write a short description.

____

____

1. Benita visited Japan with her parents. She sent this postcard to her friend Soniqa. Read what she says about her trip.

Monday, 12 December

Dear Soniqa

The stamp shows you what the weather is like in Japan right now. The country is very beautiful and you really do see women wearing traditional kimonos like the ones on the stamp.

Yesterday we went to Mount Fuji or Fuji-san as the locals call it. It is very different from the Blue Mountains because it's all alone and mostly covered in snow. We couldn't climb it as you can only climb it in the summer months.

Tomorrow we are going on a trip on the bullet train through an underwater tunnel to another island.

I can't wait!

Missing you!

Benita

a. Is Benita experiencing summer or winter? How do you know? __________

____

b. What is a kimono? __________

c. What is the local name for Mount Fuji? __________

d. Are tourists ever allowed to climb Mount Fuji? __________

e. What do you think a bullet train is? __________

____

 SKILLS: Write a description. Read and answer questions about a postcard.

2. Ricardo visited Paris, France, with his family. He took these photographs while he was there.

It gets so cold you can ice-skate on this outdoor ice-rink and the ice doesn't even melt.

This is the Eiffel Tower. It was very cold and wet when we went to see it.

This is the entrance to the Louvre Museum. It snowed while we were inside.

These are ice and snow statues at the winter market on the Champs Élysées.

a. Work with a partner. Read the captions and discuss what you can see in each photograph.

b. Use information from the photographs and the captions to write a postcard from Ricardo to his friend Ricky.

SKILLS: Read captions and analyse photographs. Write a postcard.

3. Read this tourism information brochure for people wanting to visit New Zealand.

GREAT SIGHTS, FRIENDLY PEOPLE, GOOD WEATHER, UNIQUE PLANTS AND ANIMALS – WE HAVE IT ALL.

New Zealand is a small country made up of two main islands. It has a population of only 4 million people, so it is uncrowded and ideal for people looking for peace and relaxation. But it's also attractive to those looking for thrills and adventures.

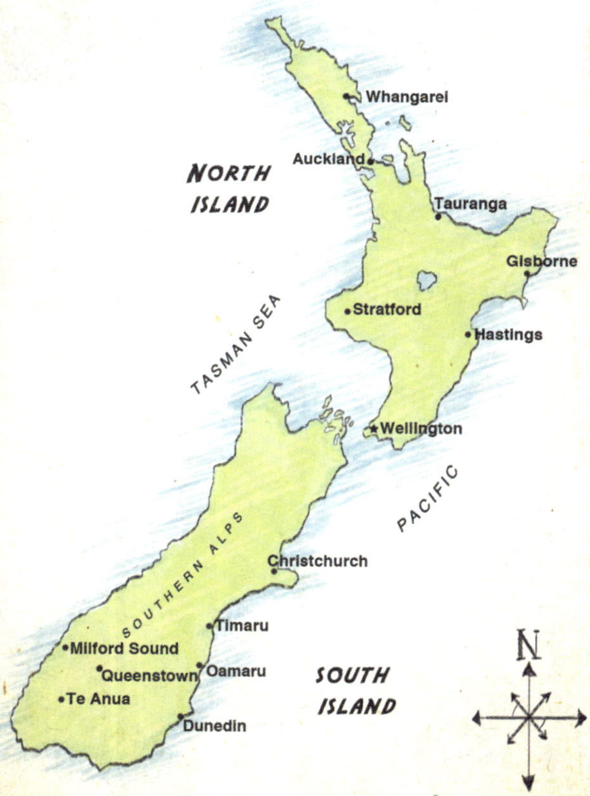

Geography

In New Zealand you can see glaciers, fiords, rugged mountains, vast plains, rolling hillsides, subtropical forest, volcanic plateaus and miles of coastline with sandy beaches.

Our location on the Pacific Rim of Fire means we also have geothermal springs and volcanoes. Lake Taupo was formed during one of the biggest and most destructive volcanic eruptions in the world. At Rotorua you can see geothermal activity close up with spouting geysers, hot-water pools and bubbling mud pools.

The 15 000-kilometre coastline has its own unique sights. On the west, the coast is wild and untamed, while on the east there are sandy beaches and harbours dotted with islands.

Weather and climate

New Zealand is in the temperate climate zone. In the far north, the weather can be quite subtropical during summer, while in the far south of the South Island it can get as cold as –10 °C in winter. The rest of the country's climate is somewhere in between, with mild temperatures, moderate rainfall and plenty of sunshine.

Visitors should remember that the weather can change very quickly. In New Zealand we say, “You can experience four seasons in one day.” The country is surrounded by ocean, and cold fronts and tropical cyclones can blow in and bring sudden changes in temperature with wind and rain. New Zealand’s average rainfall is quite high – between 640 mm and 1 500 mm. While this produces lush rainforests and is good for farming, it also means that you can get wet. We’re not called the land of the long white cloud for nothing!

Things to do

- **Take a hike.** Walk through rainforests, along golden-sand beaches, at the foot of mountains and up mountains. You can walk for half an hour, half a day or for days at a time.
- **Go for a paddle in a kayak**. Explore the dark waters of an ancient fiord or the sun-filled calmness of bays in the south. Get a thrill with a white-water rush or lift your soul while swimming with dolphins.
- **Dive or snorkel** and explore life under water. The Poor Knights Islands are known as one of the world’s best dive sights.
- **Go bungy jumping.** We invented this adventure sport. Tie an elastic rope around your feet and dive off a bridge. We’re quite sure you will love it.
- For the less adventurous, New Zealand offers a huge **variety of shopping opportunities**, from exclusive designer stores and malls to small local arts and crafts markets.
- If you are not too tired, take part in the **lively nightlife** and visit cafés, bars and top-class restaurants. You can even take in a concert or a show.

4. Imagine you are a travel agent. How would you answer the following questions from clients who want to visit New Zealand? Use the brochure on pages 56–57 to help you answer the questions.
   a. What type of weather can I expect if I travel to New Zealand in the summer months?
   b. I'd like to go hiking in New Zealand. Is there anything I should know?
   c. I love water sports. What does New Zealand offer in this area?
   d. My sister and I would like to take part in some adventures and extreme sports while on holiday. What could we do in New Zealand?
   e. I want to spend a lot of time on safe, sandy beaches with my family. Which coast should I visit?
   f. I've heard you can visit hot springs and have a mud bath in New Zealand. Where can you do this?
   g. My dad says you can experience four seasons in one day in New Zealand. What does this mean?
   h. I want a holiday with nature and outdoor activities, but I'd also like to go shopping and have fun at night. Does New Zealand offer that kind of holiday?
   i. What packing advice can you offer me for a trip to both the North and South Island in winter?

5. New Zealand and Jamaica are both island countries. Complete this table by filling in three similarities and three differences between the two countries.

Comparing Jamaica and New Zealand	
Similarities	**Differences**
1.	1.
2.	2.
3.	3.

 SKILLS: Answer questions. Complete a comparative table.

6. Work with a partner. Prepare a dramatic reading of this poem.

The useless umbrella
by Ilse Badenhorst

I got a very large umbrella
from a rather handsome fella.
It really was a lovely gift
and gave this cloudy day a lift.
But as the rain began to fall,
the umbrella did not work at all
and soon enough it was clear to me
why this umbrella was for free!

Now the frogs are making me dizzy
and my long hair is going all frizzy
and if that isn't bad enough
I've caught a cold; I'm in a huff!
Achoo, achoo, I sneeze and sneeze
That fella really was a sleaze!

Onomatopoeia
When you use words that sound like the thing they are describing, you are using onomatopoeia. For example, the poet uses the word achoo to describe a sneeze.

7. Below is a list of onomatopoeic words.
   a. Say each word aloud.
   b. Write down two things that could make each sound. The first one has been done as an example.

hiss	a snake	the air escaping from a tyre
knock		
splat		
pop		
boom		
croak		
swish		
howl		
crunch		

12 Life in the polar regions

Before you begin

- Work with a partner. Read these words. Circle the ones that mean cold.

torrid chilly blazing balmy frozen icy sub-zero
sweltering frosty boiling glacial roasting nippy polar
scalding toasty wintry arctic tropical cool

- Arrange the words you have circled from the least cold to the coldest.

____

____

1. There are many idioms and expressions that use the word cold.
   a. Work with a partner. Read these expressions. Discuss what each one means.
   b. Write a sentence below each expression to show that you understand what it means. The first one has been done as an example.
      - I don't like John, he's a cold fish.
        I tried to greet John, but he ignored me.
      - I was going to jump, but I got cold feet.
        ____
      - My teacher can be very cold-hearted if you don't do your homework.
        ____
      - When I heard the news, my blood ran cold.
        ____
      - The gang shot the security guard in cold blood.
        ____
      - My brother always pours cold water on my ideas.
        ____
      - I asked her to go with us, but she is blowing hot and cold.
        ____
      - I'm cross with her, so I am giving her the cold shoulder.
        ____
      - My granny's hands are always cold, but she says, "Cold hands, warm heart."
        ____
      - I'll get him back for this, but revenge is a dish best served cold.
        ____

 SKILLS: Identify and order synonyms. Read, interpret and write the meanings of expressions.

2. Read this information about a person who lives in one of the coldest parts of the world.

Life in Siberia

My name is Chagook. I live in Siberia in the far north-eastern part of Russia. My family is mostly nomadic, so we move around from place to place according to the seasons.

The furs I am holding come from white polar foxes. I set traps to catch the animals and then I sell the skins. My father and my grandfather were both hunters and they taught me the tricks of the trade. We sell the furs to traders from Moscow. They sell them on to be used in the fashion industry.

Fur is not as popular as it used to be because people think it is cruel to kill the animals, so we make less money than we used to. I am a bit worried that we will no longer be able to survive like this and I don't know what else we can do.

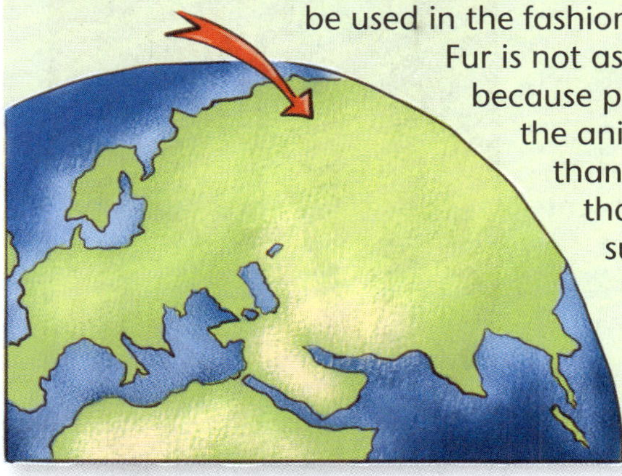

3. These questions are based on the extract. Answer them in full sentences.
   a. Where is Siberia?
   b. What does nomadic mean?
   c. Why do you think this family moves according to the seasons?
   d. What does Chagook do for a living?
   e. How did he learn how to do this?
   f. Why is Chagook concerned about his job?

4. Describe the clothing that Chagook is wearing. Read your description to your partner when you have finished.

5. Read what Robbie says about living in Canada, another cold region.

Life near the Arctic circle

Hi, I'm Robbie and I live in the far north-west of Canada, up near the Arctic circle. I work for a large timber company as a lumberjack. It's my job to cut down trees in the company's pine plantations. Most of the trees are used to make paper or wood pulp. Once I chop down the tree, we cut off the branches and saw the trunk into large logs. These logs are hauled to the river and then floated downstream to the sawmill.

I like my job, but conditions are really tough in the winter months. It's frozen all the time and it hardly ever gets light, so we work much less, which also means less pay. My company is very environmentally conscious, so they plant new trees to replace the ones that are cut down. I think this is mostly because our government has laws to make them do this. But generally, people do seem to be more aware and they know that we have to conserve the forests and care for the planet.

6. Answer these questions about Robbie's life in full sentences.
   a. Where does Robbie live?
   b. What does he do for a living?
   c. Why are conditions tough in the winter months in north-west Canada?
   d. How are the logs transported from the plantation to the sawmill?
   e. What does the logging company do to care for the environment?

7. Look at the picture of Robbie again.
   a. What does Robbie use to cut down the trees?
   b. What safety equipment does he have? List the equipment and say why each thing is necessary in his job.

 SKILLS: Read an information text. Answer questions. Analyse a picture.

8. The trees in the polar regions are well suited to the cold conditions in those regions. Read the information and study the diagram and the labels to learn more about how the trees are suited to the climate.

Natural vegetation in the frigid regions of the world

These regions are home to the world's natural coniferous forests. Coniferous trees are those that bear cones, such as pines, spruces and firs.

The diagram shows a typical conifer and the ways in which these trees are adapted to the cold climate in which they grow.

9. Complete this table to compare coniferous forests with rainforests. Go to pages 48–53 to find information on rainforests.

	Coniferous forests	**Rainforests**
Where they occur		
Type of climate they are suited to		
Description of trees found there		

SKILLS: Read an information text. Study a diagram. Read labels. Complete a comparative table.

10. Look at the two photographs below, which show traditional life in Alaska, and then answer the questions.

A traditional Inuit igloo. People live in these homes made from ice.

An Inuit boy ice-fishing. The fishermen cut holes in the ice and try to catch fish swimming below the ice.

a. What do you think it would be like to spend a night in an igloo? Write a diary entry of such a night.

b. How is ice-fishing in Alaska different to fishing in Jamaica? Write a paragraph comparing them.

 SKILLS: Analyse photographs. Answer questions. Write a diary entry. Write a comparative paragraph.

11. It is not only traditional people who live in igloos. Today many people travel to Norway to stay in a hotel built each year entirely from ice. Read the information and look at the photographs of the ice hotel in Norway.

Norway's ice hotel

For the 25th year in a row, we will build our fabulous ice hotel in Lapland during the winter of 2012. Our hotel has grown from its humble origins as a large igloo to a sophisticated structure with separate rooms all made entirely of ice and snow.

It may be winter outside, but in here it's warm and snug. Why don't you come and joir the fun this year?

12. Work with a partner to design an advertisement to attract people to the ice hotel. The theme of the advertisement should be: "Be cool. Come to the ice hotel!"

Be cool. Come to the ice hotel!

13 Anansi stories

Before you begin

- Before you read the story, answer these questions.
  - What kind of creature is Anansi? ______
  - What is your favourite Anansi story? ______
  - Circle the words you would use to describe Anansi.

shy | lazy | clever | tricky | timid | honest | greedy | cunning

1. Read this story on your own.

Anansi and Snake

There was a time when Tiger was the king of the forest. Tiger lilies were named after him, Tiger moths were named after him and stories of the forest were called Tiger stories.

Anansi was a nobody. When the animals got together they used to ask each other, "Who is the strongest animal?" And all the animals would shout, "Tiger!"

Then they would ask, "Who is the weakest?" And everyone would shout, "Anansi!" and laugh.

Anansi got sick and tired of this. One day he met Tiger in the forest. Now Tiger was much too important to bother talking to a speck of a spider, but Anansi spoke up bravely and said, "Tiger, I wonder if you would allow just one thing to be named after me?"

"What do you want named after you?" asked Tiger, looking down his nose.

"I want the stories," replied Anansi. "I want them to be called Anansi stories."

"All right," said Tiger with a haughty flick of his tail. "If you capture Snake and bring him to me, all the stories will be called Anansi stories from now on."

Anansi, who was very small, but very cunning, had no idea how he would capture Snake, who was very big. But he agreed to do it.

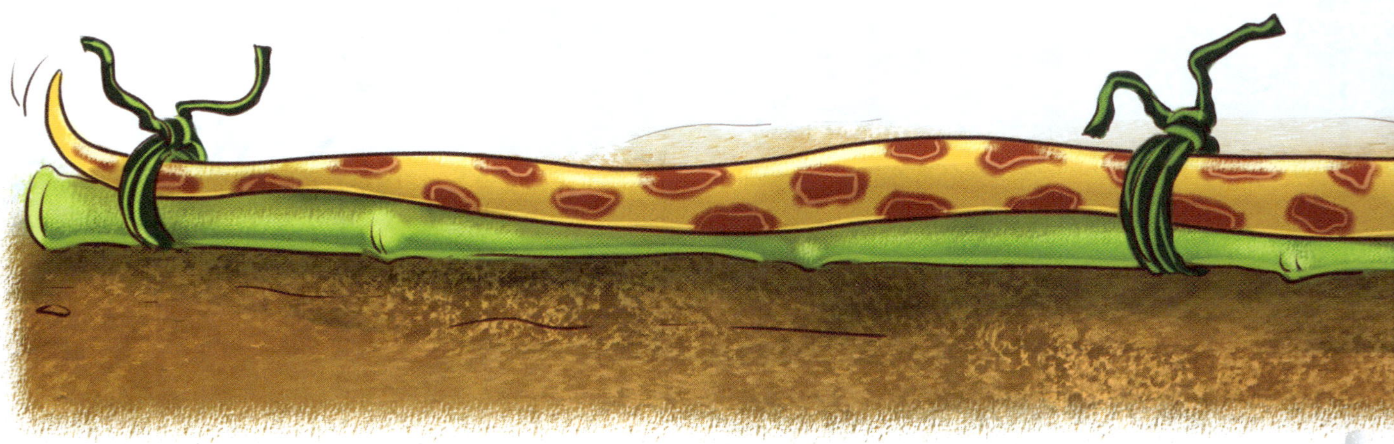

 SKILLS: Answer questions. Read a story.

First he made a noose out of strong vine and laid a trap in the forest, which he baited with berries. But when Snake came to eat the berries, Anansi found he was too weak to pull the noose closed, so Snake escaped.

Every day that week Anansi persisted with various traps. He dug pits and he made cages out of sticks. He tempted Snake with ripe bananas, mangoes and a fat piglet, but nothing worked! Snake knew that Anansi was trying to trap him and he always managed to escape.

Anansi was starting to get desperate, but at last he thought of a plan. He went and sat right in the middle of Snake's yard.

"But you bright, eeh?" said Snake who was very surprised to see Anansi sitting there. "All week long you trying to catch me, and now you sit here barefaced in my yard?"

"It's true," said Anansi. "I was trying to catch you, but for your own good. Now all the animals in the forest will continue to talk about you behind your back."

"What you talking about, Anansi?" asked Snake.

"Well, I should not be telling you this, but all the animals are saying that you believe you are the longest animal in the forest, that you think you are God's gift to 'longness'. They are saying that even the shortest bamboo is longer than you!"

"Well measure me, man!" shouted Snake. "Cut down the longest bamboo and I will teach 'em about long!"

So Anansi cut down the longest bamboo he could find and Snake, who was very gullible, lay his body along its length. Anansi tied Snake's tail to one end with strong vine.

"Stretch, Snake, stretch!" called Anansi. And Snake sweated and stretched till his eyes were squeezed shut. Quick as a flash Anansi tied Snake to the bamboo at his middle and his head. When Snake opened his eyes, he realised what had happened.

And this is how Anansi captured Snake and why from that day to this, the stories have been called Anansi stories.

2. Write the letters of the sentences below in the correct order to retell the story of Anansi and Snake.
   a. At last Anansi went to Snake and told him that the other animals were laughing at him behind his back.
   b. Anansi agreed, although he didn't know how he was going to do it.
   c. Anansi wanted the Tiger stories to be named after him.
   d. He made many different traps, but Snake escaped from them all.
   e. Anansi tied Snake to the bamboo pole and took him to Tiger to claim his reward.
   f. Tiger told Anansi that he would have to capture Snake if he wanted the stories to be known as Anansi stories.
   g. Snake stretched his body along a bamboo pole to prove that he was really the longest creature.

   ____

3. Find these words in the story and see if you can work out their meaning from the way they are used. Write the meaning next to each word.
   - persisted: ______________________
   - gullible: ______________________
   - haughty: ______________________
   - cunning: ______________________

4. Draw lines to match the descriptions on the right to the three main characters in the story.

	persistent
Tiger	haughty
	foolish
Anansi	powerful
	cunning
Snake	gullible

 SKILLS: Sequence a story. Define words. Describe characters.

The moral of a story
The moral of a story is the lesson that the story teaches us about life.

5. Put a tick next to the moral that best fits the story "Anansi and the Snake".
   - ☐ The story teaches us that some animals are very stupid.
   - ☐ The story teaches us that it is not right for any one creature to have all the power.
   - ☐ The story teaches us that we can succeed if we use our brains in a difficult situation.

6. In the story we read that Anansi tried many different ways to trap Snake; none of which were successful.
   a. Read the story again and underline the different things that Anansi tried.
   b. Use the story frame below to write about one of Anansi's attempts in more detail. This flow chart will help you with the writing process.

plan → write a rough draft → swap with a friend → edit → rewrite → copy out neatly

Story frame	
Paragraph 1 What trap did Anansi make? What did he use to bait the trap?	
Paragraph 2 What happened when Snake saw the trap? What went wrong with the trap? How did Snake escape?	

7. Read this story with a partner.

Anansi and the moss-covered rock

Once upon a time Anansi was walking through the forest when he saw a strange, moss-covered rock.

"How interesting!" said Anansi to himself. "Isn't this a strange moss-covered rock?"

Suddenly ... KABOOM! Everything went black and Anansi fell down, fast asleep.

When he woke up, Anansi rubbed his spinning head and wondered what had happened to him. "I was walking along this path," he reminded himself, "something caught my eye and I said to myself, 'Isn't this a strange moss-covered rock?' and then ..." KABOOM! Anansi fell down *again* and woke up about an hour later.

"Aha! I know what is happening," said Anansi to himself. "This is a magic rock and every time someone comes along and says the magic words, 'Isn't this a strange hmm-hmmmmm hmmmm?', down they go. I know just how to use magic like this!"

So Anansi went walking through the forest until he came to Tiger's house. Tiger had a lovely spread of food laid out and he was just about to eat. Anansi was hungry, but he was too lazy to go and find his own food, so he said to Tiger, "Tiger, I'm just going for a walk in the lovely, cool forest. Don't you want to come? It's terribly hot today."

"Yes, I'd love to come," said Tiger and the two creatures went walking through the forest together. After a while, Anansi led Tiger to a certain place.

"Tiger! Do you see what I see?"

"Oh yes, Anansi! Isn't this a strange moss-covered rock?"

KABOOM! Down fell Tiger and away ran Anansi to Tiger's house, where he made off with all Tiger's food.

Soon Anansi was tricking all the animals in the forest. Whenever he was hungry, he persuaded an animal to go to the moss-covered rock, got them to say the magic words and ... KABOOM! they fell down fast asleep. Anansi could then help himself to their food. Anansi couldn't eat all the food, but he stored it away in his house so that he'd have food for a long, long time.

What Anansi did not know is that he was being watched by quiet Little Spotted Deer. She hid in the forest and watched as Elephant, Jaguar, Snake, Fruit Bat and even Turtle were tricked out of their food by the lazy Anansi. She decided to put a stop to Anansi's nonsense.

Little Spotted Deer collected a basket of sweet coconuts and waited for Anansi to come along and invite her to go with him for a walk in the cool forest. Little Spotted Deer did not have to wait long. She agreed to go for the walk and soon she and Anansi were at the strange moss-covered rock.

"What is this?" said Anansi, pretending to be puzzled by the rock.

"What is what?" asked Little Spotted Deer.

"This!" said Anansi pointing at the rock. "Can't you see it?"

"I can't see anything," said Little Spotted Deer.

"Surely you can see it!" said Anansi, starting to get angry. "Look where I'm pointing!"

"There is nothing there!" answered Little Spotted Deer.

Anansi stomped his thin legs. "Of course you can see it! You just don't want to say it!"

"Say what? What am I supposed to say?" asked Little Spotted Deer.

Anansi shouted, "You're supposed to say, 'Isn't this a strange moss-covered rock?'!"

KABOOM! Down fell Anansi.

Little Spotted Deer ran to call all the animals and they went straight to Anansi's house. They took back all the food that he'd stolen from them and didn't leave him a scrap to eat.

An hour later Anansi woke up and rubbed his head. When he got home he found it as empty as it had been before his trickery. But if you think he learnt his lesson, you are mistaken. He's still out there playing tricks to this day ...

8. Sumarise these sentences and place them in the correct order to plot the story of "Anansi and the strange moss-covered rock".
   - First he tricks Tiger and takes his food.
   - But Little Spotted Deer sees what Anansi is doing and she decides to put a stop to his trickery.
   - One day Anansi finds a magic rock.
   - Anansi himself falls down fast asleep and all the animals go to his house to recover their stolen food.
   - Anansi discovers that every time he says the words, "Isn't this a strange moss-covered rock?", he falls down fast asleep.
   - Then he tricks many other animals in the forest.
   - She pretends she can't see the rock.
   - Anansi decides to use the magic rock to trick the animals and steal their food.
   - This makes Anansi so angry that he shouts out the magic words himself.

The structure of a story

Most stories have this structure:
- there are characters in a setting
- the characters experience a problem
- the problem is solved.

9. Set out the structure of the story "Anansi and the moss-covered rock". Use this frame.

Who are the main characters? What is the setting?	
What problem does Anansi cause for the animals?	
How is the problem solved?	

 SKILLS: Order sentences to plot a story. Identify and write the structure of a story.

10. Think of another Anansi story that you know well. Work with a partner and use the frame on page 72 to discuss whether your stories also fit this pattern.

11. Imagine that Anansi wants to trick Monkey with the strange moss-covered rock. Fill in the missing words to show what happens.

One day Anansi saw that Monkey had collected a whole pile of sweet mangoes. He decided to play ______________________________.

"Hello, Monkey," said Anansi. "Don't you want to ______________________________?"

"______________," said Monkey. So Anansi took Monkey to ______________________________.

"______________________________?" asked Anansi when he saw the ______________.

"______________________________" said Monkey.

KABOOM! Monkey ______________ and Anansi ______________.

12. Complete the sentences below to compare the two Anansi stories you have read.
    a. In what ways are the stories the same?
        - The setting for both stories is ______________________________
        - In both stories Anansi is shown to be a ______________ character.
        - Both stories show Anansi playing ______________ on other animals.
    b. In what ways are the stories different?
        - In the first story Anansi is shown to be ______________, but in the second story he is shown to be ______________________________
        - In the first story Tiger is shown to be ______________, but in the second story he is shown to be ______________________________
        - The ending of the first story shows Anansi ______________, while the ending of the second story shows ______________________________

13. The word KABOOM! in the second story is an onomatopoeic word which describes a big explosion. What onomatopoeic words can you think of to describe the following things.
    a. The sound made by an elephant squashing a ripe watermelon.

       ____

    b. The sound made by coconuts falling onto the sand.

       ____

    c. The sound of a thin stream of water falling over a rock.

       ____

    d. The sound made by Anansi's legs as he runs over dry leaves.

       ____

SKILLS: Discuss the structure of a story. Complete a paragraph. Compare stories. Write onomatopoeic words.

14 Jamaican stories

Before you begin

- Before you read the story, answer these questions about Martha Warren Beckwith.
  - When was she born and when did she die?
  - What did she do?
  - Who first brought the stories to Jamaica?

1. Read this information about Martha Warren Beckwith and then answer the questions.

Martha Warren Beckwith (1871–1959)

Many of Jamaica's folktales were written down by an American scholar and folklorist called Martha Warren Beckwith. She wrote down hundreds of folktales in a book called *Jamaican Anansi stories*. The book was published in 1924. Before she recorded these stories, they only existed in oral form.

Stories were the only possession that the slaves could bring with them on the hazardous journey across the sea from Africa. These stories were passed down from parents to children for many generations.

Many of the tales were Anansi stories, but some were about people and other creatures. The story you will read on page 75 was told to Martha Warren Beckwith by Etheline Samuels, who lived in Claremont, St Ann.

a. What words in the text tell us that these old stories were not written down until the book was published?

b. What word in the text tells us that Martha Warren Beckwith wrote down many stories?

c. Find another word in the text that means the same as:
- wrote down: ______
- stories: ______

d. Find the word hazardous in the text. What do you think it means? Tick the right answer.

long ☐ dangerous ☐ boring ☐

e. What do we call a text like the one about Martha Warren Beckwith? Tick the right answer.

an autobiography	☐	a biographic sketch	☐
a biography	☐	a folktale	☐

bio – means life (so a biography is a story about someone's life)
auto – means self (so an autobiography is a life story that was written by the person themselves)
sketch – a short piece of writing

2. Before you read the folktale below, discuss these questions with a partner.
   a. Do you know any other stories about peas, beans or seeds?
   b. What does make a fortune mean?
   c. How do you think the pea will make a fortune in this story?

3. Read this folktale that was told to Martha Warren Beckwith by Etheline Samuels.

The pea that made a fortune

One day an old lady was travelling on the road and she picked up a green pea and she planted it. And after it grew, her goat ate it off. She cried upon the goat and told it that she wanted the peas. The goat said that he didn't have anything to give her, but she could take one of his horns. She took the horn and went to the riverside to wash it. The river took it away from her. She cried upon the river, and the river said it didn't have anything to give her but a fish. She went further. She met a man who was very hungry. She gave the man the fish. After the man ate it, she cried upon the man. The man gave her a moreen. She went a little further and saw a cowboy. She gave him the moreen. After he had worn it out, she cried upon him for it. He said he didn't have anything to give her but his whip. She went a little further and saw a man driving cows. She gave the whip to the man. After the man had lashed it out, she cried upon him, so he gave her a cow; and from the cow she made her riches.

moreen – a heavy woollen cloth
lashed – to whip

4. The story uses some unusual phrases. Rewrite these phrases in Standard English.
   a. ate it off ______________________
   b. she cried upon ______________________
   c. worn it out ______________________
   d. lashed it out ______________________

5. Use these pictures to summarise the story. Write a sentence below each picture.

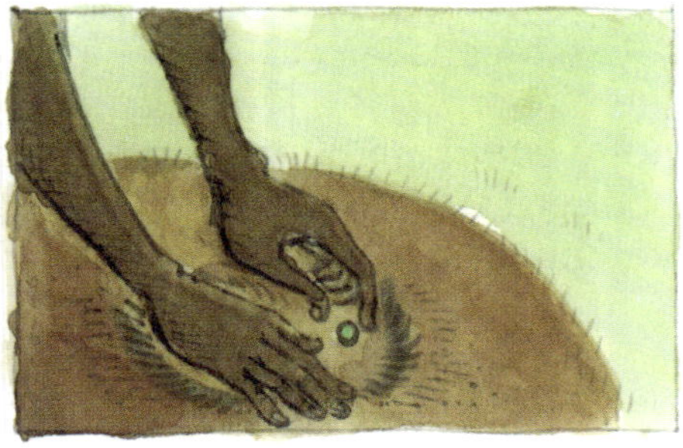

1. ______________________________

2. ______________________________

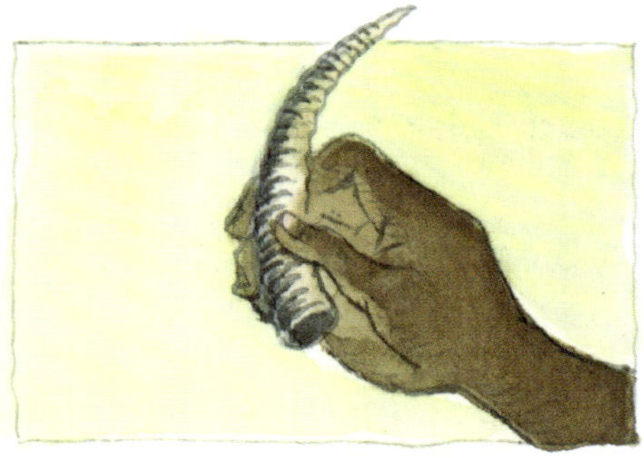

3. ______________________________

4. ______________________________

5. ______________________________

6. ______________________________

7. ______________________________

8. ______________________________

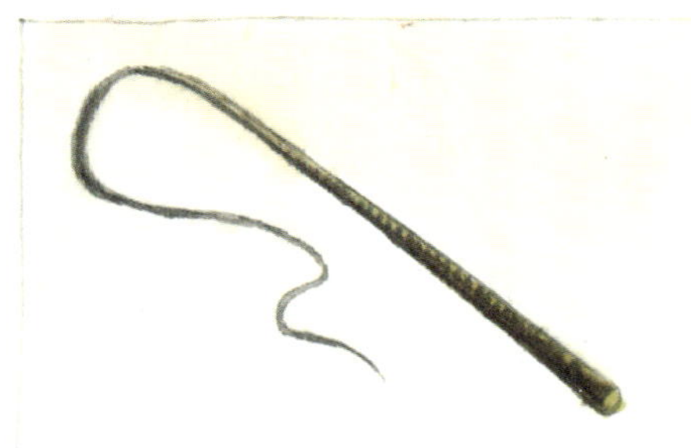

9. ______________________________

10. ______________________________

11. ______________________________

6. Write your own tale about how you traded something you had for something you really wanted. Follow these steps.
   - Give your story a title.
   - Then start as set out below and follow the pattern of the story on page 75.
   - Write a draft first and make sure all your trades make sense.
   - Write your final story on a clean sheet of paper.

Title: ____

One day I was walking along the road wishing I had a ______________. I put my hand in my pocket and found a pencil. Outside the school gates I saw a small girl. She was crying. "I can't do my homework because I have lost my pencil," she wept. I gave her my pencil and she was so relieved that she gave me ____________________

7. Read this story about the River Mumma.

The River Mumma and the Golden Table

Everyone knows about the River Mumma, who lives in the deep, green pools of Jamaica's rivers. Sometimes, people say, she rises out of the river to sit on a rock and comb her beautiful long, black hair. "But," everyone warns, "you should never look at her or touch her or she will put you in a trance and drag you by your heel under the water, where you will be sure to drown. And if you try to catch her, her children, the fish, will disappear and the river will run dry."

And everyone knows too that buried in her deepest pool is the splendid Golden Table. This table was made by the Spanish many centuries ago when they came looking for gold and riches. The River Mumma guards her table jealously.

Sometimes the Golden Table rises to the surface of the river, but should anyone try to steal it, they will get dragged into the river and will never be seen again.

One day Bastian and his sister Lora were walking home at high noon, when they saw sitting on a rock the River Mumma herself. As they stood and stared, the magnificent Golden Table rose dripping out of the water and hovered, gleaming in the light.

"Run!" called Lora, who knew what happened to those who tried to steal the precious golden prize.

But Bastian had been hypnotised by the beauty of the treasure and fell under its spell.

"Come away, Brother! Come away!" pleaded Lora and she tried to pull him by his arm. "You know what happens to greedy people who try to take what is not theirs!"

"Greedy?" said Bastian. "I'm not greedy! I'm not like Papa's boss! I wouldn't stop paying someone for their hard work in the sugar cane fields just because I felt like it!"

"I know you wouldn't," said Lora. "But remember what Mama said, 'People who are covetous end up making problems for themselves!'"

"That's true," said Bastian. "But people who don't fight for what is right get taken advantage of, like Mama was when her boss gave her a basket as her only payment for all the housework that she did."

The children continued to argue like this – and soon it was night time, the moon rose and the Golden Table sank slowly back under the water and disappeared.

As they walked home, still arguing, they were overheard by their Papa's boss, who was also walking home by moonlight.

"Where did you see this Golden Table?" asked the boss. "I think I should try and get it for myself."

"Why is that?" asked Bastian.

"Because the rich always get richer," said the boss. "That is the way the world works."

The next day the boss insisted that Bastian take him to the spot in the river where he'd seen the Golden Table the day before. Bastian pointed out the place and ran away before he could fall under the table's enchantment again.

Well, nobody ever saw that boss again, for he never came back from the river that day. The boss's son took over from his greedy father and paid the workers a fair wage for their work in the cane fields. And Bastian and Lora became known for their hard work, their honesty and their wisdom. Their Mama and Papa had taught them well.

8. Answer these questions based on the story.
   a. What does the River Mumma do if you try to touch her?

   ____

   ____

   b. Who are the River Mumma's children?

   ____

   c. What treasure does she keep in the deepest pool?

   ____

   d. How do we know that the treasure is very old? Find a word in the story that tells us.

   ____

   e. Which country's people made the Golden Table?

   ____

   f. Choose two words or phrases from this list that describe the characters of Lora and Bastian. Write them in the table.

timid | cautious | disrespectful | hot-headed | sense of justice | stupid | honest | mean

Lora	Bastian

   g. Tick the sentence that you think best describes the moral of the story.
   - The rich always get richer. ☐
   - People who long for riches make trouble for themselves. ☐
   - People must fight for what is right. ☐

9. Read the story again. Find synonyms that mean the same as these words.
   a. magnificent: ______________
   b. precious golden prize: ______________
   c. enchantment: ______________

10. Draw a picture of what you think the River Mumma looks like.

SKILLS: Answer questions. Select words that describe characters. Identify the moral of a story. Identify synonyms. Draw a picture.

11. Imagine that you are a newspaper reporter sent to interview Bastian and Lora about what they saw at the river. Complete the interview by:
    - writing the answers that you think they gave, or
    - reading the answer they gave and writing the question that you think the interviewer asked.

Question: What time of day was it when you stopped by the river?

Answer: ______________________________

Question: Very few people can claim to have seen the River Mumma. What did she look like?

Answer: ______________________________

Question: ______________________________

Answer: It was a medium-sized table made of gold and very finely crafted. It was covered with intricate patterns and was very beautiful. The table seemed to glow with a golden light. Although it looked very heavy, it seemed to be suspended in the air above the water.

Question: According to the legend, the Golden Table puts a spell on people who see it so that they cannot resist trying to steal it. Why did you not try to steal it?

Answer: ______________________________

Question: A local farmer and owner of the sugar cane field is rumoured to be missing since seeing the Golden Table. What do you think happened to him?

Answer: ______________________________

15 Folktales of the world

Before you begin

- You are going to read a story from the Democratic Republic of Congo (DRC) in Central Africa. Find this country on a map.
- Discuss these questions with a partner.
  - Look at the picture on page 83. What kind of creature is an imp?
  - What creatures are like imps in Jamaican folktales?
  - Do you think the imp will be a troublemaker or a helpful character in this story?

1. Read this story with a partner.

Outwitting the imp

Once upon a time a man cleared a piece of land and his wife planted cassava seeds while their son played nearby. They all loved fresh cassava bread baked from the roots of the cassava plant.

One day the husband and his wife visited their cassava farm. They were shocked to discover that wild animals had pulled out nearly all the roots and chewed and trampled the cassava. They decided the man would dig a large pit with a trap cover. Then the wild animals that came to steal would fall into the pit and be trapped.

The next day, while the man was digging the hole, an imp – a fearful creature of the forest – jumped from the trees. The imp said, "Well now! I will help you dig the pit, and you will share with me the animals that fall into the trap." The imp added, "All the male animals that fall into the trap will be yours, but all the female ones will be mine."

The man felt that he had to agree, or else he might be killed. After the man and the imp had dug the pit, they went home.

The following morning the man, his wife and the imp all went to look in the pit. They found one male pig in it, which the man took according to their agreement. Every morning they went to check the trap and it was always the same – male pigs, male buck and male buffaloes were caught in the trap. There were never any female animals.

The man took the animals home. His wife said, "We have plenty of meat now, but we still have no cassava bread to eat with it. There must be some cassava roots left in the soil. Tomorrow I will go and dig up what I can find and make some bread."

 SKILLS: Discuss and answer pre-reading questions. Read a story.

So early the next morning, the woman took her basket and her hoe and went to the farm, leaving her husband to look after their little boy. When the woman had been gone for some time, the boy began to miss his mother.

His father decided they would go to the farm and visit her there. As they drew near, they heard the imp gleefully singing, "Oh my! Oh my, at last I have a female animal in the trap!"

When the boy and his father looked into the trap they were horrified to see the mother looking up at them from the bottom of the pit.

"All the female animals that fall into the pit are mine!" said the imp, greedily rubbing his hands together.

The boy knew that he had to do something to save the situation.

"Father," he said, "you made the agreement. You were to have all the male animals and the imp was to have all the female animals that fell into the trap. We have had plenty of animals. Let him take this one!"

The imp grinned. "This is a wise boy!"

While the father was still speechless at what his son had said, the imp jumped into the trap to claim his prize. No sooner had he done so than the boy called out, "Father, look! There is a male animal in the trap! It is yours!"

On dropping down into the trap the imp had become, according to his own agreement, a male animal in the trap. As a result, he belonged to the man. The imp, to save himself, had to give up his claim to the woman. And this is how the boy outwitted the imp and saved his mother's life.

cassava – an edible tuber that looks like a long potato
outwit – to use your brains (or wits) to trick someone

2. Find the following words in the story. Then use each word in a sentence of your own that shows its meaning.
   a. gleefully: ______________________________
   b. bargain: ______________________________
   c. horrified: ______________________________
   d. speechless: ______________________________

3. Imagine that the boy in the story wrote a letter to his friend to tell him about what happened with the imp and how he saved his mother's life. What would he write?

 SKILLS: Write sentences to show the meaning of words. Write a friendly letter.

16 A tale from Russia

Before you begin

- The name Natasha is Russian. List two other things you associate with Russia.

  ____

  ____

- Discuss stories about stepmothers with your partner.
  - Do you know any other stories about evil stepmothers?
  - Are all stepmothers evil?
  - Suggest a reason why stepmothers are often portrayed as evil in stories.
- Make five new words with the letters in stepmother.

  ________ ________ ________ ________ ________

1. Read this story.

Baba Yaga

Once upon a time an old man, a widower, lived in a little hut in the forest with his daughter Natasha. They were very happy together until the old man decided to marry again.

The stepmother hated Natasha. She made her do all the housework and complained about her to her father. The foolish old man believed his new wife.

One day the stepmother decided on a plan to get rid of Natasha forever. She waited for a day when Natasha's father was not at home.

"You must go to my sister Baba Yaga and ask her for a needle and thread," the stepmother told Natasha.

"How will I find her?" asked Natasha very fearfully, for she knew that children who went to Baba Yaga's house never returned.

The stepmother pinched Natasha's nose. "This is your nose," she said, "follow it and you will find her." She gave Natasha some dry bread and cheese and scraps of meat wrapped in a handkerchief for the journey.

Natasha did not dare disobey her stepmother, so she followed her nose through the forest and eventually she came to Baba Yaga's house. It was surrounded by a high fence made of bones.

Natasha pushed open the gate and the hinges went CR-E-E-E-AK like the rickety bones of a very old person. Natasha noticed a rusty oil can lying on the ground and she poured a little oil onto the gate's hinges.

Inside the fence was the strangest house she had ever seen – it stood on long, bony chicken legs and walked around the yard. Natasha also saw a servant girl weeping as she tried to sweep the dirty yard. "Here, take my handkerchief," said Natasha. The servant girl took the handkerchief and blew her nose and smiled gratefully at Natasha because people were seldom kind to the girl at Baba Yaga's house.

Natasha noticed a thin dog that was gnawing on an old bone under a bush. Her kind heart felt sorry for the dog so she gave him her stale bread and scraps of meat. The starving dog gobbled them up in an instant.

Natasha reached the door of the strange house and knocked.

"Come in!" said a croaky voice. Natasha opened the door and there sat Baba Yaga, the bony-legged one. She smiled at Natasha with her iron teeth while weaving on a loom near the window. In the corner sat a thin cat watching a mouse hole.

"Excuse me," said Natasha and she tried to keep a steady voice, "your sister has sent me to ask you for a needle and thread."

"Did she now, my pretty one?" said Baba Yaga and she flashed her iron teeth. "You come over here and sit down at my loom and weave for me while I go and fetch a needle and thread."

So Natasha sat at the loom and began to weave.

Baba Yaga went straight to the servant girl. "Go and fill the bath with hot water. I'm going to scrub that little girl very clean and then I'll make her into a nice little dinner, I will."

Natasha overheard what Baba Yaga said and when the servant girl came inside to fetch the jug to fill the bath, Natasha pleaded with her to use a sieve and take as long as possible to fill the bath. The servant girl said nothing, but she did take a very long time to fill that bath.

While Baba Yaga was out of the room, Natasha spoke to the cat that was watching the mouse hole. "What are you doing?" she asked.

"I'm watching for a mouse," said the cat, "for I have not had any dinner for three days."

"Luckily I have some cheese left," said Natasha and gave the hungry cat the small piece of cheese that she had in her pocket. The thin cat pounced on the cheese and ate it all up.

Then the cat whispered to Natasha, "There is a comb and a towel on the stool that you are supposed to take to the bath house. Take them and run away! When Baba Yaga chases after you, throw the towel on the ground and it will turn into a wide, enchanted river. This will delay her progress for a while. When she gets across the river, you must throw the comb on the ground and it will turn into a thick tangle of enchanted forest. Baba Yaga will never get through that enchanted forest. Now run for your life!"

Natasha thanked the cat with all her heart. Then she picked up the towel and comb and ran for her life!

2. Make a list of all the kind acts Natasha did at Baba Yaga's house.

3. Because Natasha had been so kind, she received a lot of help to escape from Baba Yaga's house. Write down what you think happened next in the story. Include how the gate and the dog helped her.

4. Find the following words in the story. Draw lines to match each with its meaning.

widower	a frame for weaving cloth
disobey	old and shaky
rickety	a man whose wife has died
loom	to not do as you are told
delay	to slow down

5. You have already written an ending for the story, now read the ending that the author wrote.

Baba Yaga (*continued*)

Natasha's kindness was rewarded because as she ran past the dog, it did not bark and as she ran through the gate, it did not squeak. Natasha escaped into the forest, but Baba Yaga soon discovered what had happened.

Baba Yaga jumped into her giant mortar and, beating the air with her pestle, she flew over the forest until she saw Natasha running for her life through the trees.

mortar and pestle – a stone jar and a grinder for crushing spices

"You'll never escape from me!" Baba Yaga screeched and she started to swoop down from the sky to catch Natasha.

Natasha, thinking quickly, threw the towel onto the ground and it was just as the cat had promised: a wide, enchanted river grew from the towel. Baba Yaga knew that she would never be able to fly over the enchanted river, so she gnashed her iron teeth and flew back to her house to fetch a herd of cows.

She drove the cows to the river. "Drink! Drink!" she shouted at the cows and they obediently drank up the enchanted river. Baba Yaga quickly got back into her mortar, tucked her bony legs under her chin and flew after Natasha.

Natasha heard the screech of her laughter from the sky. As she looked up fearfully, she saw Baba Yaga speeding towards her. Luckily Natasha still had the magic comb in her pocket. She threw it on the ground and a thick tangle of enchanted forest sprang up around her.

Baba Yaga realised that she had been defeated and, screaming with rage, she flew back to her strange house that stood on bony chicken legs.

Natasha finally arrived home safely and fell into her father's arms.

"Where have you been?" asked the old man. Natasha told him everything that had happened. When her father heard that the stepmother had plotted to send his own precious daughter to be eaten by Baba Yaga, he was very angry. He chased the stepmother out of the house and told her never to return.

From that day he took great care of his daughter and they went back to their happy life together.

6. Tick the sentence that you think best describes the moral of the story.
   - If you do kind deeds you will get help when you need it. ☐
   - Stepmothers are always horrible to children. ☐
   - Children should always do as they are told. ☐

7. a. Write a paragraph describing Baba Yaga. You can get some clues from the story or you can make up your own ideas. Think about these things before you write your description.
      - Is she thin or fat?
      - What does her skin look like?
      - What does her hair look like?
      - What are her teeth like?
      - What do her legs and fingers look like?
      - How does she move?

   b. Next draw a portrait of Baba Yaga.

SKILLS: Identify the moral of a story. Write a descriptive paragraph. Draw a portrait.

17 Cars

Before you begin

- Work with a partner. Discuss the answers to these questions.
  - What is your favourite make of car? Why?
  - Which make of car seems to be the most popular in Jamaica? Why?
  - What is the longest journey you have taken in a car?
  - What did you enjoy about the journey? What did you not like about the journey?

1. There is one car for every 23 people in Jamaica. In the USA and the UK there is one car for every 2 people.
   a. What do these statements mean? Talk about this with your partner.
   b. Draw a diagram to show this information. You can use symbols, pictures or graphs in your diagram.
   c. In Cuba, there is one car for every 574 people. What does this tell you about Cuba? Talk about this with your partner.

2. Look at this diagram carefully. It shows how long the same journey took at different times.

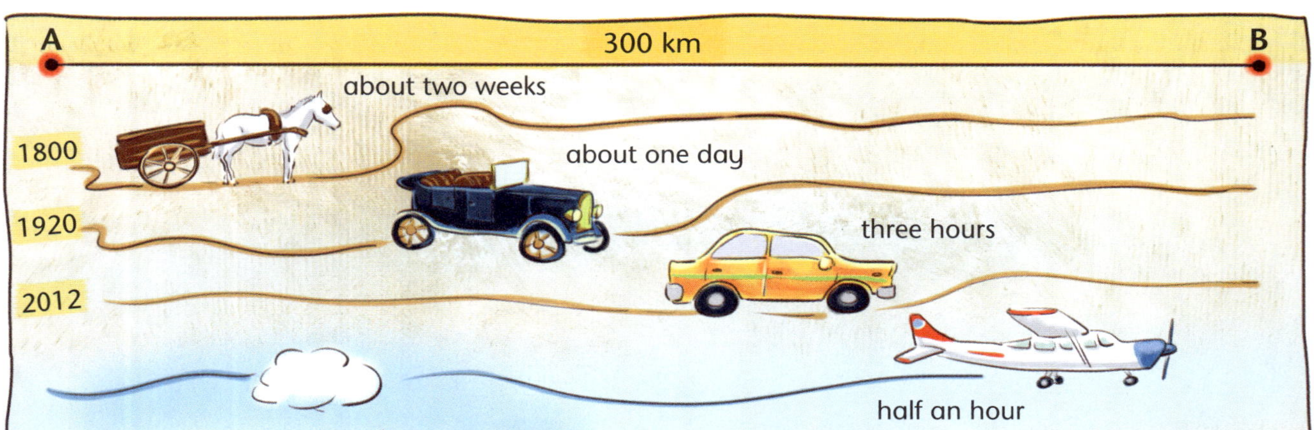

   a. How long did it take to travel 300 km in 1800? ______
   b. Why did it take less time to travel this distance in 1920? ______
   c. How long does it take to travel this distance by car today? ______
   d. Why is it much quicker if you travel by aeroplane? ______

 SKILLS: Answer questions. Interpret statements. Draw a diagram. Analyse a diagram.

3. Work with a partner. Read this poem aloud. Take turns to read the verses. Illustrate the poem in the space provided.

My car is constructed of pickles
by Kenn Nesbitt

My car is constructed of pickles.
It's wonderfully crunchy and sweet.
If ever I'm hungry while driving
I pull off a pickle to eat.

The engine is made out of gherkins.
The dashboard's an extra-large dill.
The windows and wipers are kosher
as well as the bumpers and grille.

The hood's made of hamburger slices.
The gas tank is brimming with brine.
The doors are delectably salty.
The stick shift is simply divine.

There's one little problem I'm having.
I'm sure you would know what I mean
if ever you saw this contraption;
my marvellous pickle machine.

I guess I've included my auto
in just a few too many meals
and now it won't budge when I start it;
it seems I have eaten the wheels.

4. Answer these questions about the poem.
   a. Which two lines in each verse end with a rhyming word? ____________
   b. Give another name for these car parts.
      - hood: ____________
      - bumpers: ____________
      - gas tank: ____________
      - stick shift: ____________
   c. The poet's car is made out of food. What are real cars made from? Write a list of five materials you would find in a modern car. Next to each one, say which part of the car is made from this material.

5. Read this information about the invention of the earliest petrol-powered cars.

Karl Benz and Gottlieb Daimler

The first petrol-powered motor car was invented in 1885 by a German engineer named Karl Benz. Benz's car was a three-wheeler, which he called the "Motorwagen". The car was designed from scratch to be lightweight and safe.

The Motorwagen had a water-cooled engine, powered by gasoline. But as there were no gas stations at that time, they had to use a fuel called ligroin that you could only buy at a chemist shop.

Benz thought the three-wheeled design was the most efficient and easiest to steer. The problem was that old roads had two deep grooves in them from all the horse-drawn carts, so there were lots of accidents when the front wheel of the car got stuck in a groove.

The Motorwagen

In the same year, 1885, another German engineer called Gottlieb Daimler invented a new petrol-powered engine. He fitted this engine to a wooden bicycle to make a vehicle. This was in effect the first motorcycle.

The first motorcycle

Did you know?

Although Gottlieb Daimler invented the modern motor car, he did not actually like to drive. One biography says that he never ever drove himself, although he was a passenger on at least one journey before his death.

In 1886, Daimler made his first car. He fitted his high-speed engine to an old-fashioned horse-drawn carriage. This saved money because he did not have to design a car to fit the engine. He simply fitted his engine into an existing vehicle. Daimler's horseless carriage was soon much more popular than Benz's Motorwagen because it was cheaper and it could travel at higher speeds.

Daimler's horseless carriage

Daimler was an engineer at heart. His goal was to produce a gasoline-powered engine that could be used in all sorts of vehicles. He worked with an existing engine design, which was for large engines, until he was able to make an engine small enough to fit into his horseless carriage. This engine had 1.5 horsepower – in other words, it worked as hard as one and a half horses. Today a medium car has an engine that works as hard as 250 horses.

In 1926, the Benz and Daimler motor car manufacturing companies joined up to form a new company called Daimler Benz, which existed until fairly recently and which became most famous for its Mercedes Benz motor cars.

Did you know?

The name Mercedes Benz came about when a young Austrian businessman bought into the Daimler Benz company. One of the conditions of his deal was that the new cars would be named after his daughter Mercedes.

6. a. Do some research and then complete this table to compare Benz's Motorwagen with a modern Mercedes Benz.

	The Motorwagen	A modern Mercedes Benz
wheels		
body		
interior		
safety features		
speed and reliability		

b. Imagine you were one of the first people to take a short trip on Daimler's motorised wooden bicycle. Write a diary entry to describe your experience.

7. Bertha Benz (Karl Benz's wife) was the first person to take a long-distance journey in one of these early cars. Read the information about her journey on page 95. As you read, remember that this was the first petrol car, so no one had seen anything like it. There were no gas stations or even proper highways. The car must have been quite a sight as it made its way through small towns and rural areas.

 SKILLS: Do research. Complete a comparative table. Write a diary entry. Read information.

A trip of a lifetime

On 5 August 1888 Bertha Benz and her two sons set off on a 160 km journey to visit relatives. Bertha left a note to tell Karl where she was going and, with no permission from the authorities, she set off. Her main aim was to prove to Karl that the car worked and that it would be popular if people got to see it.

However, the journey turned into an adventure and Bertha had to overcome several problems. No one sold petrol at that stage, so she had to buy ligroin to power the engine – this was only available at pharmacies. The chain of the car broke, so she needed to find a blacksmith. The brakes failed and had to be repaired. (Bertha's repair in fact led to the invention of brake linings.) The fuel pipe got blocked and Bertha had to clear it with her hairpin. She also had to use one of her garters to insulate a wire. The journey took her from dawn to dusk to complete, and despite the perils and adventures, she drove home again the next day.

People along the route were terrified by the car, but Bertha did get a lot of publicity. Her experiences also allowed her to suggest improvements that were built into later models. One of these was a gear to help the car get up hills.

8. Imagine you are Bertha Benz. Complete this letter to a friend telling her about your trip.

9. What do you think Karl Benz said when he found out that his wife had taken off with the car? Work with a partner and role play a conversation that he might have had with one of his colleagues at work after he received Bertha's note.

Benz House
Mannheim
7 August 1888

Dearest Klara

You're never going to believe what I have done.

____

____

____

____

____

____

____

____

____

Yours in adventure
Bertha

10. If you want to drive a car you have to pass a driving test, get a licence and obey the rules of the road. Drivers are reminded of the rules of the road by road signs like these. Work with a partner to answer these questions orally.
    - What does each sign tell the driver?
    - Why is this important?

11. Work in groups. Read these rules of the road for drivers published by the National Council for Road Safety. Discuss how each rule helps to keep drivers and pedestrians safe.

Road safety rules

1. Do not exceed the speed limit.
2. Drive on the left of the road, unless you are about to overtake or turn right.
3. At night, drive well within the limit of your headlights.
4. Before you slow down, stop, turn or change lanes, do the following:
    - check your rear-view mirror
    - signal your intention by hand or indicator light signal
    - make sure you can do so without inconvenience to others.
5. Do not travel too closely to the vehicle in front of you (allow at least one car length, and two car lengths on wet roads).
6. Wear your seat belt.
7. All motorcyclists, including pillion riders, should wear helmets.

12. Read this information about the "red flag" traffic laws that were used in England around the time of the first petrol cars. Discuss why you think these laws were introduced.

The Red Flag Act

This law stipulates that all mechanically powered road vehicles must:

- have three drivers: one to drive, one to give power and the other to carry the red flag
- not exceed 4 mph (6 km/h) on the open road and 2 mph (3 km/h) in towns
- be preceded on foot by the driver carrying the red flag. He should wave the red flag to warn the public of their arrival.

 SKILLS: Interpret and analyse road signs. Read rules. Read and discuss information.

13. Cars have changed a great deal since the first petrol-powered cars of the 1880s. Today cars are light, fast and much safer for drivers and passengers.
    a. List three things that make modern cars safer for drivers.
    b. List three things that make modern cars safer for passengers.
    c. What do you think is the most important safety feature in a car? Give a reason for your answer.

14. Look at this drawing showing what cars could look like in the future. Work in groups to answer these questions.

    a. What traffic problems do you think we would have if cars could fly?
    b. What new rules of the road do you think we would need if cars could fly? Make a list of at least five rules.
    c. Why would we need each of these rules?
    d. What special safety features would cars need if they could fly? Make a list of at least three things. For each one, say why you think it is necessary.

18 Bicycles and motorcycles

Before you begin

- Read these statements about bicycles and cycling. Fill in the missing words. Look at the bottom of the page to see if you have filled in the correct answers.
  - ______________ bicycles can be parked in the space given to one car.
  - More than one hundred million bicycles are manufactured worldwide every ______________
  - On a bike you can travel three times faster than you can walk using the same amount of ______________
  - Lance Armstrong has won the Tour de France cycle race seven times. He is the only ______________ to have done this.
  - BMX (a type of extreme off-road ______________) is an Olympic sport.
  - Half of all the parts in a normal bicycle are in the ______________
  - The longest tandem bike ever built was around 20 m long and could seat ______________ people.
  - The world record for the slowest cycling ever was set by a Japanese man who stayed still on his ______________ for almost $5\frac{1}{2}$ hours.
  - There are twice as many bicycles in the world as there are ______________

1. Complete these sentences about bicycles. You can find all the information you need in the timeline on page 99.
   a. The first bicycles were made from ______________
   b. The first bicycle had no ______________
   c. The velocipede was also called the boneshaker because ______________ ______________
   d. The penny farthing was made from ______________
   e. The safety bike was so called because ______________
   f. Technology in the 1960s allowed the development of ______________ ______________
   g. Mountain bikes have ______________

2. Read the information in the first box on page 99. The hobby horse had neither pedals nor a chain. How do you think people rode this early bicycle? Write a short set of instructions for riding this bike.

____

____

Answers: • twenty • year • energy • person • cycling • chain • 35 • bike • cars

3. Study this timeline, which shows the development of the bicycle.

1818
Karl von Drais invents the first two-wheeler type bicycle called the velocipede or hobby horse. People struggled to balance this machine so they "cycled" by pushing off with their feet. The velocipede was popular until a law was passed that prevented people from riding on the pavements. People couldn't balance on the poor roads, so they stopped using the hobby horses.

1860
The boneshaker was made of stiff materials and it had steel wheels. Because the roads were cobbled, this bike literally made your bones shake. It had a front wheel with pedals, no chain and one large gear. It became very popular for indoor cycling in large cycling halls.

1870
The penny farthing or "high wheeler" was more comfortable than the boneshaker, but you had to be quite acrobatic to get onto it and ride it. It was made entirely of metal and the pedals were attached to the front wheel. The tyres were made of solid rubber (no tubes). This machine was the first one to be called a bicycle.

1885
The safety bike was invented by John Kemp Starley in England. This bike was safer than the penny farthing. It had a chain and pedals and both wheels were the same size. At first these bikes had hard rubber tyres, but once the "tube tyre" was introduced many people took up cycling. But because bikes were quite expensive, only wealthy people could afford them.

1960s to present
From 1890 to 1960, bicycles continued to develop. By 1960 the racing bicycle had been developed. This is a lightweight bicycle designed for fast cycling on smooth tracks or roads. Racing bicycles have light metal or carbon frames, thin wheels, small tyres with smooth tread and a narrow saddle. The handle bars are curved. The pedals have clips so the cyclist's shoes can be fixed to the pedals. At first, racing bikes had very few gears, but today they can have up to 30.

1970s to present
Mountain bikes were developed. These bicycles are designed for going off the road and cycling on rougher ground. They have strong, lightweight frames made from light metals or carbon fibre combinations. The saddle is broad and they have suspension in both wheels for comfort. The tyres are thick, with tread for grip, the brakes are strong and effective, and the handlebars are mostly straight. The modern mountain bike can go almost anywhere.

4. Study the racing bike and the mountain bike on page 99.
   a. Complete this table to compare the two types of bicycle.

	Racing bike	Mountain bike
Materials it is made of		
Wheels and tyres		
Saddle		
Handle bars		
Additional features		
Best suited to what kind of terrain?		

   b. Look at the picture below. It shows a proposed design for a racing bicycle to be used in the 2012 Olympic Games. Discuss the picture with a partner.
   c. Complete this table to compare this bicycle with an ordinary bicycle.

	Olympic concept bicycle	Ordinary bicycle
Materials it is made of		
Wheels and tyres		
Saddle		
Handle bars		
Additional features		

 SKILLS: Write instructions. Complete comparative tables. Analyse a picture.

5. Do you know how bicycle gears work? You are going to carry out an experiment to find out. In groups, read through the instructions carefully and then do the experiment.

Experiment: How do bicycle gears work?

Aim: To see what effect gears have on a bicycle's movement.

Apparatus you will need

a bicycle with gears; a tape measure; some chalk; a safe, level space (out of the traffic)

Method

1. Put the bicycle into its lowest gear.
2. Make a chalk mark on the ground next to the back tyre where it touches the ground.
3. Turn the pedals one complete turn. At the same time, walk the bicycle forward in a straight line.
4. Make another chalk mark on the ground to show the position of the back tyre now.
5. Measure the distance between the two marks. Record this distance.
6. Put the bicycle into its top gear and repeat steps 2 to 5.

a. Complete these statements to show what you found out about the distance the bicycle moved in your experiment.
   - In the lowest gear the bike moved ______________________ in one turn of the pedals.
   - In the highest gear the bike moved ______________________ in one turn of the pedals.

b. Choose and underline the correct word in each pair to explain the effect that the gears have on a bicycle's movement.

The (lowest/highest) gear works as a force magnifier. It is very (slow/fast) on flat ground, but good for going up hills. The pedals go round (quickly/slowly) compared to the wheels. The (high/low) gear is for pedalling (uphill/downhill) or for going (slowly/fast) on level ground. The wheels go round (quickly/slowly) compared to the pedals, but it takes much (more/less) power to move the pedals.

6. Read this cartoon strip story about a young boy learning to ride a bicycle.

 SKILLS: Read a cartoon strip.

7. Answer these questions about the cartoon strip in full sentences.
   a. How does the boy feel about learning to ride a bike? Explain how you know this.

   b. What happens when he sees his dad take the training wheels off his bike?

   c. Why does the boy think the bike hates him?

   d. Do you think the bike really attacked the boy? Give a reason for your answer.

   e. Describe how the boy's facial expression changes in the last three pictures.

8. Read this verse from a poem with a partner. Underline the words you do not understand.

Instructions for learning to ride a bicycle, by Miss Frances Willard, 1895
by Evalyn Parry, based on words by Frances Willard

Strange as this paradox may seem
You will do this best by not trying to do it at all
You must quickly make up your mind
Or as quickly, be cast in yonder mud puddle.

Two things must occupy your thinking powers
To the exclusion of every other thing:
First the goal
Second, the momentum required to reach it!

   a. Use a dictionary to find the meanings of the words you did not understand.
   b. Describe the kind of bicycle that Miss Willard would have ridden.

   c. She says the best way to learn to ride a bike is by "not trying to do it at all". What do you think she means?

   d. Work with your partner. Discuss the method that you think is best to teach someone to ride a bicycle. Tell another pair about your method and listen as they tell you about the method they would use.

SKILLS: Answer questions. Identify difficult words. Use a dictionary. Write a description. Have a discussion.

9. Read this extract from an Internet blog. It was written by a motorcycle racer.

22 March

Safety first!

Yes folks, that is me shortly before I bit the dust, or the tarmac track in my case. And yet, here I am, writing my blog, only one short day later. What is my secret? Am I indestructible? Well, the simple answer is: I'm not, but my safety gear is. And I never leave home without it.

Motorbike racers need to wear protective gear. If you've ever watched a race you'll have noticed that the riders all wear a racing suit, a helmet, gloves and boots. The helmet is by far the most important piece of safety equipment, but if you are racing, you need a good suit as well.

Today's suits are made from incredibly strong materials such as Kevlar, nylon or leather. It's my suit that has allowed me to hit the ground, slide across the track and get up and walk away, bruised and embarrassed, but largely undamaged. My suit has built-in gloves with carbon fibre pads to protect my knuckles and fingers. It also has lightweight titanium pads built in to protect my knees, elbows and shoulder. I wear padded, closed boots to protect my feet and ankles.

As I said earlier, for any motorcyclist, the helmet is the most important piece of equipment. A good helmet consists of two layers: a hard outside shell and an inner, padded layer to cushion and protect your head. I prefer a full-face closed helmet and I always have a visor. My helmet was expensive, but I reckon it is worth it – it has saved my life on numerous occasions. Buy the best you can afford and never, never get on a bike, even a small one, without a helmet.

10. Read the blog on page 104 again. Then study this picture, which shows a motorcyclist dressed in safety gear.
    a. Add labels to the picture.
    b. Complete the information boxes to say why each piece of equipment is important.

Why is this necessary?

Why is this necessary?

Why is this necessary?

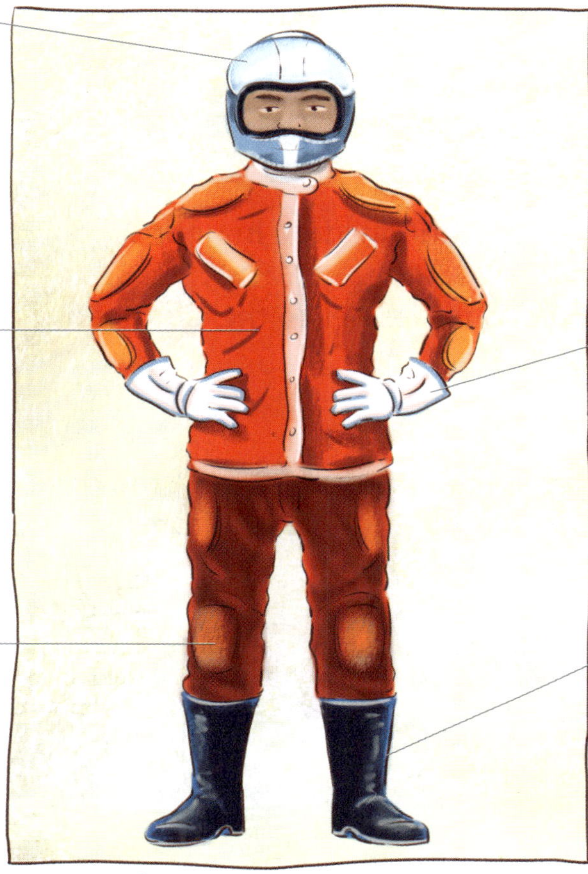

Why is this necessary?

Why is this necessary?

11. You have been asked to prepare a short radio commercial to raise awareness and encourage people to wear helmets when riding any kind of bike. Complete this mind map to show what points you would include in your commercial.

Why wear a helmet?

19 Other vehicles

Before you begin

- Make a list of the different types of vehicles that are found in your local area.

- Name three types of vehicles that children in your school use to get to school.

- How do goods from other countries get to the Caribbean?

1. Look at this diagram showing the main stages in the development of vehicles. Write a caption below each section of the diagram.

 SKILLS: Make a list. Answer questions. Analyse a diagram. Write captions.

2. Look at the different vehicles in the picture. Beneath each one, write two things that are likely to be transported in this kind of vehicle.

3. Read what each person says about travelling by bus or taxi.

Mrs Randal: I love travelling by bus. It's clean, safe and cheap, and I can read while I go from place to place.

Jerome: I like taxis – they are fast, easily available and quite cheap.

Mrs Randal: I disagree. Minibus taxis are overcrowded and the drivers go too fast. I think they are dangerous.

Jerome: I don't like the bus. The service is not reliable and you have to wait ages for a bus. Our buses don't have safety belts, so you can easily get hurt in an accident.

4. Complete this table by writing all the advantages and disadvantages that you can think of for these types of transport.

	Advantages	Disadvantages
bus		
taxi		
private cars		

5. On a visit to London, Rachel and her family travelled by train. They saw these signs at the station in London.

a. Match the pictures to their meanings below. Write the letter of the picture next to its meaning.

telephone ☐ restaurant ☐ lost property ☐ way out ☐

waiting room ☐ coffee shop ☐ ticket office ☐

information ☐ taxi rank ☐ toilets ☐

b. Why do you think stations and airports use pictures and symbols like these rather than written signs?

____

____

6. Here is a train timetable for trains running from London to Edinburgh. Discuss the questions that follow with your partner.

Station		Mon–Thu	Fri	Sun
London Euston	departs	2350	2350	2327
Watford	arrives	0010	0010	2347
Carlisle	arrives	0516	0516	0504
Carstairs	arrives	0620	0621	0620
Edinburgh	arrives	0716	0715	0716

a. How are the times set out on this timetable?
b. From which station does the train leave?
c. How often does it stop en route?
d. At what time does it get to Edinburgh most mornings?
e. On which day does the journey take the longest?
f. This is a sleeper service. What do you think that means?
g. On which day is there no train from London to Edinburgh?

7. This cartoon shows an incident that a traffic policeman had to deal with. Fill in the speech bubbles to show what you think the people (and one of the goats) are saying. You can use Standard English or Jamaican Creole.

8. Imagine you were the traffic policeman who had to deal with this incident. Write a short incident report describing what happened. Write in the past tense and use reported speech only.

Traffic Incident Report no. 221

Date: ______________________

Time: ______________________

Place: ______________________

Reporting officer: ______________________

Description of incident: ______________________

____

____

Details of any fines or citations issued: ______________________

____

____

Signed: ______________________

9. Play the Road Traffic Game on page 111 in groups of four. Each group will need a die. Read through the rules of the game before you start.

Rules

1. Each person must have a small marker to keep his or her place.
2. Put your names in alphabetical order to decide the order of play.
3. Take turns to throw the die. Move your counter the number of places shown.
4. When you land on a block with an arrow, read the instructions and follow the arrow.
5. The first person to land on or pass over block 36 is the winner.

10. When you have finished playing, think about what things can make a road journey safe and pleasant and what things can make a road journey unsafe and unpleasant. Use ideas from the game and add your own. Summarise your ideas here.

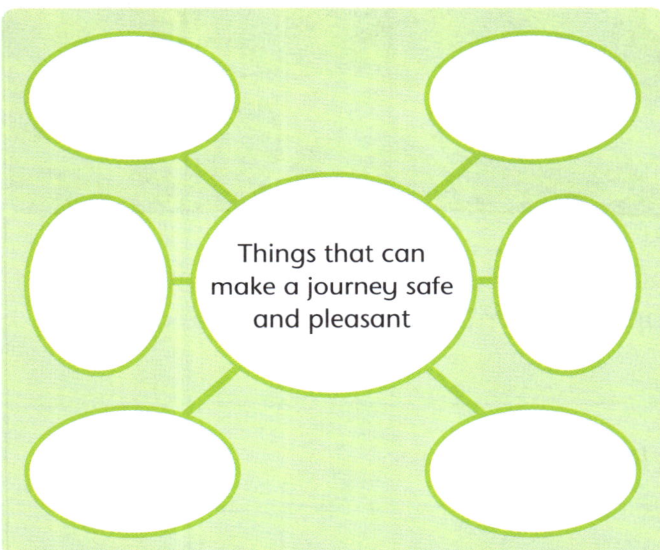

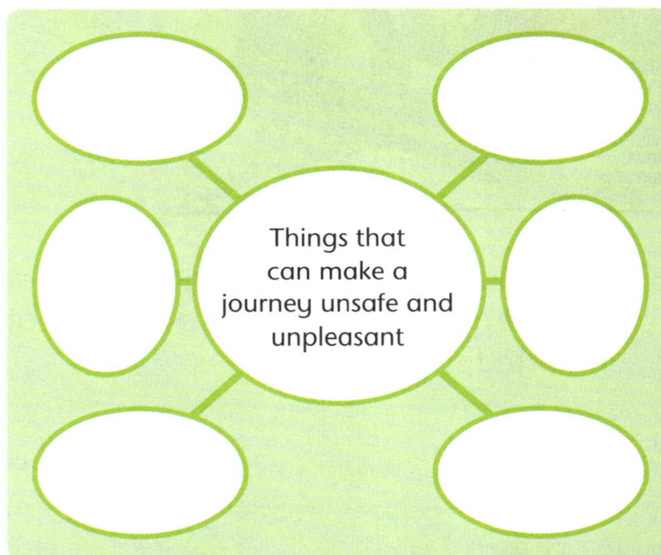

11. Write a paragraph about the journey you had as you played the game. Say whether your journey was pleasant or unpleasant and explain why.

 SKILLS: Follow instructions. Summarise ideas on a mind map. Write a description.

1
START
2
3
4 You pay the toll fee.
5 Lucky break – all green lights!
6 ACCIDENT!
CRASH
7
8
9
You meet the morning rush hour.
10
You take the bypass and skip the main road.
11
12
13
14
You use the new tunnel to save time.
15
DETOUR – burst pipe floods road.
16
The new freeway is open.
17
18
19
20
A traffic officer waves you on.
21
Taxis block the road.
22
23
Oh no – a puncture!
24
25
26
ACCIDENT!
CRASH
27
28
29
30
You meet the evening rush hour.
31
32
SPEED BUMPS!
33
34
35
36
WINNER

12. Read this page from Benita's diary. You are going to answer questions about it.

Dear diary

Today I got a new go-cart. It is very exciting and I am quite sure I am going to be a star. Just as soon as I get it into working order. But let me explain ...

My brother Milton is very good with his hands. So, with that in mind, I took it upon myself to rescue the Hope Street Gang's old go-cart, which they'd unceremoniously dumped on the empty lot on the corner.

When I looked at the go-cart I didn't see the missing wheels or the broken axle. I didn't see the ripped seat or the missing panels. I didn't even see the frayed and knotted steering rope. All I saw was a freshly painted speeding cart carrying me triumphantly to glory in the next local race.

It was quite a mission to get the cart home. I think I may have noticed the lack of wheels at that stage, but I persevered, pushing and dragging it up the block. People looked at me like I was quite mad. I was too busy sweating and struggling to really take any notice.

When I got the cart home, Milton wasn't there. My mum took one look at it, raised her one eyebrow and said, "Why you drag dat ole wreck home? What you gone do wit it?"

"I'm going to race it," I said, as if it was the most obvious thing in the world.

"Tchhh," my mum said, turning around to go inside. "Don you go be leavin that in my front yard. Neighbours gon tink we gon mad."

I just sighed. Clearly my mother could not see the potential that I saw in this magnificent racing machine.

a. Where did Benita get her new go-cart? ______

b. Was it in good condition? How do you know? ______

______

c. How did Benita get it home? ______

______

d. Was her mother pleased to see it? How can you tell? ______

______

13. Imagine you are Milton. Complete the following conversation between Milton and his sister Benita.

Benita: Oh Milton, I am glad you are home.
Milton: ______
Benita: I have a new project for us to do together.
Milton: ______
Benita: Well, I found this great go-cart and I thought we could fix it up. Look, here it is.
Milton: ______
Benita: Oh come on, Milton, it's not that bad.
Milton: ______
Benita: I think you are exaggerating a bit.
Milton: ______
Benita: Please, please, please …
Milton: ______

14. Milton decides to fix up the go-cart. Imagine you are Benita. Complete this diary entry telling about the first time you took the go-cart out for a ride.

Dear Diary

Today was the best day ever. I finally ______.
The only problem was, I didn't know how to ______

It was a bit of a disaster when ______

In the end I had to ______

Teacher's notes

General information

The following notes are intended only for the lessons that require additional support or instruction. Please consult these pages if you are looking for guidance for a particular lesson. Notes are not provided for every single lesson.

Reading comprehension is the ability to understand text and interact with it in a meaningful way. Strong reading comprehension skills are needed to read in this way and to interpret many different aspects of life.

The following aspects all rely on strong reading skills:

- understanding content in all subjects
- achieving good marks in tests
- finding information easily
- enjoying reading
- reading effectively.

It is therefore vital to begin building a solid foundation for reading comprehension from a young age.

The Hodder Comprehension course explores many types of texts and is designed to help pupils systematically master all essential reading comprehension skills. The course recognises that written responses to reading greatly enhance comprehension. Reading various types of texts helps pupils learn language and text structures they can use in their own writing. Therefore, many comprehension exercises in the course are extended to include various forms of written work.

The heading of the pre-reading activities in each lesson is *Before you begin*. What the pupils bring to the lesson, determines how they understand what they read. The *Before you begin* activities aim to expose the pupils to new vocabulary, draw on previous experience and create a greater interest in, understanding of, and involvement in the topic. This in turn improves comprehension.

Skills table

TERM 1 UNIT 1 POEMS	
LESSON	**SKILLS**
1 **Animal poetry**	• Discuss a familiar poem. • Read and interpret poems. • Compare poems. • Answer questions. • Justify opinions. • Define words. • Write questions. • Identify young animals. • Read and modify instructions. • Perform a poem.

2 Figures of speech	• Say, identify, interpret and write examples of alliteration. • Read and write similes. • Analyse and compare photographs. • Read a poem. • Make comparisons. • Answer questions. • Identify similes and metaphors. • Justify a choice.
3 A story poem	• Learn and recite a verse. • Draw a picture. • Skim read biographical information. • Answer questions. • Read and discuss a limerick. • Draw a picture. • Complete a limerick. • Read a lyrical story poem. • Complete sentences. • Write descriptions. • Answer questions using adjectives.
4 Writing poetry	• Read and complete a poem. • Read advice. • Develop a checklist. • Identify syllables. • Read and write syllable poems. • Read and write haiku. • Read a cinquain. • Answer questions. • Complete cinquains. • Express an opinion.
TERM 1 UNIT 2 SPORTS	
5 Playing ball	• Discuss different ball games. • Read an information text. • Write true statements. • Complete a timeline. • Identify and write meanings of homonyms. • Read a newspaper article. • Answer questions. • Justify an opinion. • Read website information. • Design a logo and write a slogan. • Write questions.
6 Cricket	• Interpret cartoons. • Read information texts. • Write a fact file. • Interpret a pie chart. • Conduct a survey. • Complete a tally table and a pie chart. • Write a summary. • Read a letter to a newspaper. • Identify examples of facts, opinions and exaggeration. • Answer questions. • Read an information text. • Interpret a map and information text. • Write a description.

7 **Track and field**	• Interpret pictures. • Categorise information. • List words in alphabetical order. • Match words and definitions. • Skim read an information text. • Answer questions. • Read information. • Write the meaning of words. • Complete a wordsearch. • Make sentences. • Identify true and false statements. • Interpret a table. • Write questions. • Write crossword clues.
8 **Sport at school**	• Match information. • Read a notice. • Write and answer questions. • Design a flag and write a slogan. • Read, interpret and find solutions for problems. • Discuss and write rules. • Write a letter.
TERM 2 UNIT 1 LIFE ACROSS CLIMATIC ZONES	
9 **Climates around the world**	• Discuss questions. • Read, interpret and answer questions about a climate graph. • Discuss the meaning of words. • Complete tables. • Write descriptions. • Interpret a climate graph. • Read and interpret a map and climate graphs.
10 **Life in the tropics**	• Identify animals. • Read and write facts and fact files. • Read and interpret a diagram and photographs. • Categorise statements as true or false. • Read an interview. • Compile a list. • Answer questions. • Write an explanatory paragraph. • Read a review.
11 **Life in the temperate regions**	• Write a description. • Read and answer questions about a postcard. • Read captions and analyse photographs. • Write a postcard. • Read a brochure. • Answer questions. • Complete a comparative table. • Read and dramatise a poem. • Explore onomatopoeia.

12 Life in the polar regions	• Identify and order synonyms. • Read, interpret and write the meanings of expressions. • Read an information text. • Answer questions. • Write and read a description. • Analyse a picture. • Study a diagram. • Read labels. • Complete a comparative table. • Analyse photographs. • Write a diary entry. • Write a comparative paragraph. • Design an advertisement.
TERM 2 UNIT 2 FOLKTALES	
13 Anansi stories	• Answer questions. • Read a story. • Sequence a story. • Define words. • Describe characters. • Identify the moral of a story. • Use a story frame to write about an event. • Order sentences to plot a story. • Identify, write and discuss the structure of a story. • Complete a paragraph. • Compare stories. • Write onomatopoeic words.
14 Jamaican stories	• Skim read. • Answer questions. • Read biographical information. • Answer pre-reading questions. • Read a story. • Write phrases in Standard English. • Summarise a story. • Follow steps to write a tale. • Select words that describe characters. • Identify the moral of a story. • Identify synonyms. • Draw a picture. • Complete an interview.
15 Folktales of the world	• Discuss and answer pre-reading questions. • Read a story. • Write sentences to show the meaning of words. • Write a friendly letter.
16 A tale from Russia	• Discuss and answer pre-reading questions. • Read a story. • Make a list. • Predict and write an ending for a story. • Match words and meanings. • Read the ending of a story. • Identify the moral of a story. • Write a descriptive paragraph. • Draw a portrait.

TERM 3 UNIT 1 ALL ABOUT VEHICLES	
17 Cars	• Answer questions. • Interpret statements. • Draw a diagram. • Analyse a diagram. • Read a poem. • Identify rhyming words. • Write synonyms. • Write a list. • Read information. • Do research. • Complete a comparative table. • Write a diary entry. • Complete a friendly letter. • Role play a conversation. • Interpret and analyse road signs. • Read rules. • Read and discuss information. • Analyse a picture. • Compile lists.
18 Bicycles and motorcycles	• Extend vocabulary. • Complete sentences. • Read and interpret a timeline. • Write instructions. • Complete comparative tables. • Analyse a picture. • Read instructions. • Do an experiment. • Read a cartoon strip. • Answer questions. • Identify difficult words. • Use a dictionary. • Write a description. • Have a discussion. • Read a blog. • Analyse and label a picture. • Write information. • Complete a mind map.

19 Other vehicles	• Make a list. • Answer questions. • Analyse a diagram. • Write captions. • Interpret pictures. • Read opinions. • Identify advantages and disadvantages. • Interpret and match signs. • Read a timetable. • Write speech bubbles. • Complete an incident report. • Follow instructions. • Summarise ideas on a mind map. • Write a description. • Play a game. • Read a diary entry. • Read and complete a conversation. • Write a diary entry.

Lesson-by-lesson information

TERM 1 UNIT 1 POEMS

1 Animal poetry (pages 2–7)

The pupils develop their vocabulary and reading comprehension skills by discussing, reading, interpreting and comparing poems and reading and modifying instructions. They answer questions, define words, justify their opinions and identify young animals. They also write questions and perform a poem.

page 2: Introduce this unit by showing the pupils various poetry books. Leave the books on display and encourage the pupils to read poems when they have time. Briefly discuss poetry and explain how it is a creative form of literature that expresses feelings, ideas and stories. There are many different types of poems. Poetry does not have to be serious and can be fun to read and write. Encourage the pupils to start their own poetry anthology in which they write and decorate some of their own poems as well as favourite poems written by other people, either classmates or published poets. Working on a personal poetry anthology is a constructive way to keep fast workers occupied.

page 5: Before the pupils write questions to ask the poet, revise open and closed questions. Remind them that closed questions can be answered simply by saying yes or no, whereas open questions lead to further discussion. Example of a closed question: Did you enjoy writing this poem? Example of an open question: Why did you write this poem? Encourage pupils to use the words why, when, how, which, what, who and where in their questions.

2 Figures of speech (pages 8–12)

The pupils learn more about figures of speech by reading, identifying, writing and comparing examples of alliteration, similes and metaphors. They also read a poem and answer questions.

You may want to extend this activity by having the pupils work in pairs to make up their own tongue twisters, similes and metaphors about one another. Encourage the pupils to write their own poems in their poetry anthologies using alliteration, similes and metaphors.

3 A story poem (pages 13–16)

The pupils extend their reading comprehension skills by reading and interpreting biographical information, a limerick and a lyrical story poem. They also learn and recite a verse, interpret a description, draw a picture, skim read, answer questions, complete a limerick and sentences and use adjectives to write descriptions and answer questions.

Display various story poems. Read parts of them to the class to introduce and conclude lessons and encourage them to read the rest of the poem in their spare time. Encourage the pupils to write their own story poems and limericks in their personal poetry anthology.

page 13: Show the class a variety of biographies and read excerpts from them. Tell the class that biographies tell us more about someone's life and experiences. A biography is not written by the person who it is about, but rather by another person. If a person writes their own story this is called an autobiography.

Revise how to skim read. Remind the pupils that when they skim read they quickly scan the page, ignoring detail and information they do not need. Skim reading gives an overview of what the extract is about and can also help them find the answers to questions.

page 14: Have the pupils highlight the answers in the information text and number them according to the question number before they write them down.

Children love to listen to, write and read limericks, so read various limericks to them and give them time to write their own, which they can then read to the class.

page 15: Explain that the words "lyrical story poem" tell us that "The owl and the pussycat" is a story poem that is told in a song-like way.

4 Writing poetry (pages 17–21)

The pupils learn more about different types of poems by reading, interpreting, answering questions about and writing syllable poems, haiku and cinquains. They also read information about how to write a poem, develop a checklist, complete syllabification activities and write an opinion.

Have various haiku and cinquains available to read to the class. Encourage the pupils to write their own haiku and cinquains in their poetry anthology.

page 18: Discuss the value of checklists. The pupils need to understand that checklists help them stay focused and minimise careless errors. Let pupils refer to their checklist when they write their own poems in this lesson.

page 19: The pupils should recognise that each line of "The cloud" has one syllable more than the previous line. Each line of "Holidays" has one syllable less than the previous line.

TERM 1 UNIT 2 SPORTS

5 Playing ball (pages 22–27)

The pupils develop their reading comprehension skills and vocabulary by reading information texts and a newspaper article, and writing true statements, meanings of homonyms, answers to questions, a slogan and questions. They also complete a timeline, design a logo and justify an opinion.

Display both fiction and non-fiction books about sports throughout this unit. Introduce the unit by reading an extract from a fiction and non-fiction book about sport. Have the pupils identify from which type of book you are reading. Discuss the difference between fiction and non-fiction. Fiction refers to novels about imaginary people, places and events. Non-fiction texts are factually correct. Show the class examples of a biography, an autobiography and factual books about sports or a sportsperson.

pages 22–23: Ask the pupils to identify in which type of book this text may appear.

page 25: If you would like to extend this activity, have the pupils find sports articles in the newspaper. They should read the article and then tell their group members about it. Alternatively, have them write articles about talented sportspeople or a sporting event at their school.

page 26: Discuss logos and slogans. Show the class some logos and slogans, and discuss whether or not they are effective. They should understand that slogans are short, catchy, memorable phrases.

If you would like to extend this part of the lesson, have the pupils do research about charities and non-profit organisations related to sport. They should share the information they read with the class. Have them discuss what sort of organisation they would like to support if they had a lot of money.

6 Cricket (pages 28–33)

The pupils develop their vocabulary and reading skills by reading and interpreting information texts, a pie chart, a letter to the newspaper and a map. They also interpret cartoons, give an opinion, conduct a survey, identify facts, opinions and exaggeration, and write a fact file, summary, answers to questions and a description.

page 28: Display autobiographies and biographies of cricket legends in class. Introduce and conclude lessons by reading extracts from the books. Encourage the pupils to read the books.

page 30: Ask the pupils what the purpose of a survey is: a survey is a data-gathering tool that collects information about people. Draw the pupils' attention to the pie chart. Explain that it looks like a pie with different size slices. The size of the slice depends on how much or little it represents. Use an example from the chart to help them understand this concept.

page 31: To reinforce the concepts introduced, have each pupil share a fact, opinion and exaggeration about someone in their class – remind them to be polite and kind! You may wish to extend this activity by giving each pupil a newspaper and asking them to find the section in the newspaper where the letters appear. They should read the letters and then share their opinion on one of these with the class.

7 Track and field (pages 34–39)

The pupils extend their reading, writing and vocabulary skills by reading and interpreting information texts, answering questions, matching words and definitions, writing meanings of words, completing a wordsearch and writing sentences and crossword clues. They also interpret pictures and a table, answer questions, categorise information and list words in alphabetical order.

page 34: Before the pupils put the words into alphabetical order, show them different types of dictionaries. Divide the class into groups and give each group a dictionary. Let the pupils browse through the dictionaries and then discuss the value of a dictionary as a learning tool. Revise how the words are listed in alphabetical order.

page 38: Discuss the advantages of viewing information in the format of a table. Tables are orderly and focus only on key information. This makes it easy to compare information.

8 Sport at school (pages 40–43)

The pupils read and analyse a notice and problems, write questions, answers to questions, solutions, rules and a letter. They also match information, design a flag and write a slogan.

page 41: If you would like to extend this activity have the pupils write catchy songs to chant/sing at an interschool athletics meet.

page 43: Before the pupils write their letter, discuss the format and tone that the letter should have. Remind the pupils to include an introductory, main and closing paragraph.

TERM 2 UNIT 1 LIFE ACROSS CLIMATIC ZONES

9 Climates around the world (pages 44–47)

The pupils develop their reading comprehension skills by reading and interpreting graphs and maps, discussing questions and meanings of words, writing descriptions and completing tables.

Discuss the headings of the unit and lessons. Ask the pupils to describe the types of books in which they would find information about these topics. Show and display various books about the topics.

page 44: Have the pupils examine the bar graph closely and identify what information on it is key to understanding the graph. Talk about why it is usually quicker and easier to gain information from a graph than it is if the same information were written in a paragraph.

page 45: If the pupils struggle to explain the meanings of the words in activity 3, encourage them to look up the words in a dictionary and then explain the meanings in their own words.

page 47: Discuss tables and make sure the pupils understand the following:

- To complete the table accurately they must understand the information.
- They should use keywords and phrases to complete the table.
- Transferring information to a table helps you to understand and retain information and is an effective study skill.

Discuss why it is important for the columns and rows of tables to have appropriate headings.

10 Life in the tropics (pages 48–53)

The pupils use reading comprehension skills to interpret and complete a variety of activities about fact files, a diagram, photographs, an interview and a review.

page 49: The pupils will need books or access to the Internet to complete the fact files accurately.

page 51: Talk about why people are interviewed before the pupils read the interview. After they have read the interview, ask them if the interviewer asked open or closed questions. They must give a reason for their answers.

page 53: Discuss the purpose of book reviews. If you want to extend this activity, have the pupils write book reviews about a book they have enjoyed reading.

11 Life in the temperate regions (pages 54–59)

The pupils extend their reading and writing skills by reading, answering questions about and writing a postcard, reading, interpreting and answering questions about a brochure, reading and dramatising a poem, writing a description, reading a caption, analysing photographs, comparing countries and exploring onomatopoeia.

Display a variety of postcards and brochures that the pupils can read.

page 58: Before the pupils answer the questions, encourage them to read each question, highlight the information needed to answer the question in the brochure and number the information so that it corresponds with the question numbers. This is a good habit to develop, as it will help them answer questions accurately and in detail.

page 59: Discuss the purpose of a dramatic reading. The pupils are required to entertain their audience by adding expression and actions to the reading of the poem. If you would like to extend the activity, have the pupils do one of the following:

- Find examples of onomatopoeia in the comic section of the newspaper.
- Find a picture in a magazine that shows an action and then describe the picture using as many examples of onomatopoeia as possible. Display the pictures. Muddle the descriptions and read them to the class. They should then try to match each description to a picture.

12 Life in the polar regions (pages 60–65)

The pupils read, interpret and answer questions about expressions, a variety of information texts, pictures and photographs. They write descriptions, a diary entry and a comparative paragraph and also design an advertisement. They complete other relevant activities that develop their reading comprehension skills.

page 64: Remind the pupils that diary writing is informal and reflects personal feelings and happenings.

page 65: Display various advertisements. Ask pupils to identify effective advertisements and to give reasons for their selection. Discuss the qualities of effective advertisements.

TERM 2 UNIT 2 FOLKTALES

13 Anansi stories (pages 66–73)

The pupils read, sequence, plot and compare stories. They write definitions and they also write about the structure of a story and complete relevant activities that develop sound reading comprehension skills.

Discuss the title of the unit, "Folktales". Tell the pupils that folktales are stories that have been passed down orally through many generations. They become part of the community's tradition. They often have animal characters with human characteristics. Ask them to name some of the folktales they know. Show them various books of folktales. Display the books while you are working on this unit and encourage the pupils to read them. Let the pupils share enjoyable folktales with the class. If you want to extend the activity, have the pupils dramatise folktales.

page 69: Discuss the flow chart in detail before the pupils complete the activity. Recap the process of writing before any activity in which pupils are asked to write a story. This will ensure that the recommended writing process becomes a habit.

page 72: Talk about what the plot of a story is. The plot of a story refers to the events, in the correct sequence, that make up a story. Encourage the pupils to apply the usual structure of stories to all their story writing in the future.

14 Jamaican stories (pages 74–81)

The pupils develop their reading, writing and vocabulary skills by reading, interpreting and completing activities about biographical information, stories and an interview.

page 74: Show the class an autobiography. Draw their attention to the title and author and read the blurb at the back of the book. Have them identify the similarities and differences between an autobiography and a biography.

page 76: Refer to the structure of a story on page 72 and remind the pupils to consider this structure when they plan their story. Also recap the flow chart on page 69 and have the pupils follow the process while writing.

page 80: Remind the pupils that synonyms are different words that have the same meaning.

15 Folktales of the world (pages 82–84)

The pupils develop their vocabulary, writing and reading comprehension skills by discussing and completing pre-reading activities, reading and interpreting a story and writing sentences and a letter.

page 84: Before the pupils write their letter, recap the purpose and format of a friendly letter.

- Purpose: To communicate with someone you are usually acquainted with.
- Format: Address, date, greeting, introductory paragraph (in which the main reason for writing is introduced), main paragraph (in which the main reason for writing is extended), closing paragraph (which wraps everything up), closing, name.

16 A tale from Russia (pages 85–89)

The pupils extend their vocabulary and their reading and writing skills by reading and interpreting a story, making a list, predicting an ending, matching words and their meanings, identifying the moral of a story, writing a descriptive paragraph and drawing a portrait.

Page 87: Let the pupils highlight Natasha's kind acts before writing the list.

TERM 3 UNIT 1 ALL ABOUT VEHICLES

17 Cars (pages 90–97)

The pupils develop their reading, writing and language skills by reading, interpreting and completing activities about old, modern and future cars, road signs and rules of the road.

Display interesting poems and also fiction and non-fiction books about cars through the ages. Read extracts from them to introduce and conclude lessons.

page 90: Show the class various diagrams and discuss them before pupils draw their own diagram. Examples: line graphs, pictograms, bar graphs, pie charts. Remind the pupils to label their diagrams carefully so others can make sense of the information displayed on it. Divide the pupils into pairs to compare their diagrams.

page 94: The pupils may need access to information in books or on the Internet to complete the table accurately.

18 Bicycles and motorcycles (pages 98–105)

The pupils develop their vocabulary and their reading and writing skills by reading and completing activities about a timeline, pictures, instructions, a cartoon, a verse and a blog.

page 101: Plan ahead for the experiment so it can be done at school instead of for homework. Have the pupils work in pairs or groups to perform the experiment and discuss the follow-up activities.

page 102: Introduce this part of the lesson by showing the class various comics and comic strips. Discuss how they tell a story using pictures in sequence, speech bubbles and brief sentences.

page 104: If possible, show the class appropriate blogs on a computer and discuss them. Talk about blogs the pupils may read or would like to read.

page 105: If you would like to extend this activity, divide the class into groups and have them produce, practise and present their commercials to the class.

19 Other vehicles (pages 106–113)

The pupils read and interpret a diagram, pictures, opinions, signs, information, a timetable, instructions, a diary entry and a conversation, and they complete other relevant activities that develop their reading comprehension skills.

page 108: Talk about where else timetables need to be read. Examples: flight schedules, bus and school timetables.

pages 110–111: Have markers and dice available so the pupils can play the game.

page 113: Discuss the format of a dialogue before the pupils complete the conversation.